The United States, Great Britain and the Middle East: Discourse and Dissidents

Anne Murray

SOCIAL SCIENCE MONOGRAPHS, BOULDER
DISTRIBUTED BY COLUMBIA UNIVERSITY PRESS, NEW YORK
1999

Copyright © 1999 by Anne Murray
ISBN 0-88033-981-0
Library of Congress Catalog Card Number 99-71017

Printed in the United States of America

TABLE OF CONTENTS

INTRODUCTION	1
THE REAL AND THE IDEAL: AMERICA AND THE CHARTIST DREAM	10
ACROSS BOUNDARIES: WHERE HISTORICAL CONSTRUCT MEETS POLITICAL ACTION	34
VICTIMS AND STATISTICS: SUFFERING AND POLITICAL UTILITY	52
JEWISH IMMIGRATION AND A JEWISH ARMY: BRITISH AND AMERICAN APPROACHES	82
AMERICAN JEWS, THE ISRAELI LOBBY, AND 1,000 DAYS OF INTIFADA	119
BIBLIOGRAPHY	148

INTRODUCTION

I travelled in a country mapped for me by many hands since ancient times, scrawled over with names in languages not my own.[1]

The history of most countries is a palimpsest—ideas and systems and namings have been superposed over the centuries, some developing out of the history of those who live there, others imposed from outside.

The countries of the Middle East in particular have experienced a long succession of civilisations: the Punic, the Hellenic, the Roman, the Abbasid, the Ottoman, the European and finally the neo-colonial and the American. As civilisation replaces civilisation, what A. Toynbee terms "cultural aggression"[2] rarely leaves the victim society unscathed. New values and systems, new economic and intellectual patterns are introduced, a residue remaining when the victor society withdraws or another, newer, pattern is imposed. Among the strategies used to appropriate the victim society and integrate it into the victor society is the attempt to impose the stronger society's vision of its history its place and role in the world and in time.

History is thus in no way a neutral study. It is a means by which one society permeates and appropriates another. Crudely put, it enabled the French coloniser to persuade Arabs that they were part of the French story, sons of "nos ancetres les gaullois." It is now being used to persuade them that the Americans too were victims of colonisation and were thus not dissimilar from them, establishing a shared identity, a complicity of estate. Americans prefer to present themselves as colonized rather than colonizer (and, indeed, colonizers who disagreed with the mother country on treatment of the native inhabitants; compare the British colonists' fury when Britain's government, which had supported them in the French and Indian Wars and whose victory over France they had applauded, drew up the Proclamation Line of 1763, with the 20th century French colons' outraged disbelief when General de Gaulle's words "Je vous ai compris" turned out to mean he would not support them against the Algerian nationalists). This sleight of hand shown by the colonizer in appropriating "victim" status can be effective.

Indeed, history is not objective. And this has been remarked by various historians, some of whose views on the uses and abuses of history shall be cited. Marx wrote of *Capital* that the aim of his book was "to lay bare the economic law of motion of modern society" and shorten the birth pangs of the phases of its development.[3] Dialectic in its rational form "includes in its comprehension and affirmative recognition of the existing state of things, at the same time also, the recognition of the negation of that state, of its inevitable breaking up...and is in its essence critical and revolutionary."[4] Obviously this concept of historical change, with its rider that historical development could be helped along by human agency, was of vital importance for the anti-colonial movements of the 20th century. Revolutionary Marxism was a potent tool for changing a mentality (away from acceptance of the inevitability of colonization towards an awareness of the economic basis of colonialism and how it could be fought) and thus a political position.

The English historian A.L. Rowse also saw the study of history as having political implications, speaking of "the use of history, and the duty of historians, in forming an educated public opinion, particularly about international affairs."[5] His view of history, in which he saw the U.S. in 1945 as having "merited the leadership of the Western world, for its responsibility, its consideration of the interests and well-being of others, and for its unexampled generosity"[6] is interesting in its partisanship. He sees good historians (he especially recommends biographers) and bad historians (who make unscrupulous use of diplomatic notes and memoranda). Among those he praises are the American journalist historians W. Lippmann and H.S. Commager; particularly castigated is the British historian A.J.P. Taylor, whose *Origins of the Second World War* (Taylor presents Hitler as an opportunist with rational aims rather than power-mad, and the war as fought by the Allies to keep Europe the same and by Germany to change it) is described by Rowse as "a fantastic and unrecognisable picture of a profoundly serious historical theme." Rowse suggests the importance of the "correct" writing of history: (what he sees as) misrepresentation has "ill political consequences, a malign illustration of the importance and use of history in political affairs."[7] For Rowse, therefore, history should be used to promote a political agenda.

A different use of history is proposed by the English historian A. Toynbee. The study of history, carried out comprehensively and comparatively, would ensure that the human race has a future. "Mankind is surely going to destroy itself unless it succeeds in growing together into something like a single family. For this, we must become familiar with each other; and this means becoming familiar with each other's history."[8] So far, Toynbee argues, the nation-state has figured rather largely in history; Toynbee grants value to neglected areas and shows how ideas and values can change as civilisations encounter each other in space or in time. The use of this type of history would prevent the triumphalist, or progressivist, approaches often found in the teaching of British or American history and would promote, for example, the Arab/Islamic history of the Middle Eastern area.

A writer who tries to counter this triumphalist kind of history writing is the American H. Zinn. His book *A People's History of the United States* is, he says, partisan "because the mountain of history books under which we all stand leans so heavily in the other direction so tremblingly respectful of states and statesmen and so disrespectful, by inattention, to people's movements that we need some counterforce to avoid being crushed into submission." He presents the American system as "the most ingenious system of control in world history,"[9] with elite control of power and wealth to keep the enemy at bay, and with foreign wars used to unite people with Establishment. While "most histories understate revolt, overemphasize statesmanship, and thus encourage impotency among citizens," history which keeps the memory of people's resistance alive "suggests new definitions of power."[10] Zinn's especial concern is with the American people, but his conclusions could be extended to apply to foreigners who are presented with the traditional, triumphalist image of American history as a model.

This topic—"history from below," or perhaps from the victim of "cultural aggression"—was among the concerns addressed by a group of historians in *New Perspectives on Historical Writing*. The control of a people's memory, or the destruction beyond recovery of its memory, is an important political act, whether we refer to the control of the minds of one's own population or those of the people of another country. In colonial situations, where there are extremes of power and powerlessness, "accounts of social structure and of dynastic tradition are most commonly reinvented"; and in powerful industrial countries such as Britain and the U.S. embarrassing historical documents are at times destroyed. History must be "correct." In Britain, Mrs. Thatcher's government abolished the Schools Council, whose history project had "understood exactly the political significance of a robust study of history and therefore placed on the back cover of the book, the following saying of Nikita Khrushchev: 'Historians are dangerous people. They are capable of upsetting everything'." The Thatcher project aimed at imposing on the national curriculum its "triumphalist, Whiggish, document—driven and parochial syllabus of British political and constitutional history, with an emphasis on rote learning of dates and 'facts' and an aversion to the historical imagination."[11]

In the U.S., a similar attempt to doctor historical fact and destroy historical memory was made early this century. J. Lukacs describes how after 1920 states—both progressive and populist—enacted laws to censor the teaching of history. In 1921 a New Jersey law banned textbooks that "belittle, falsify, misrepresent, distort, doubt or deny the events leading up to the Declaration of Independence, or to any war in which this country has been engaged"; in 1924 a Wisconsin law forbade the "teaching of any historical facts considered unpatriotic by politicians and the people" or fact which "defames our nation's founders or misrepresents the ideals and causes for which they struggled and sacrificed, or which contains propaganda favorable to any foreign government." In a second wave of anti-Communist patriotism, after 1947, a further attempt was made to destroy independent historical thought by firing dissident historians in schools and universities. "Publicly, elite schools proclaimed their defense of academic freedom and autonomy. Privately, they cooperated with the FBI and other agencies."[12] When one considers the effect that this "historical cleansing" must have had on teaching and research, it is easier to understand how both the American people and the outside world are offered a skewed picture. One example of this is the story of how the American colonists offered the Olive Branch Petition and were snubbed by the British government—scant mention being made of British or colonial attempts to resolve the problem by compromise (Conciliation Proposition and Peace Commission, Galloway Plan). Indeed, the speedy contemporary excision of this Galloway Plan from records, and its subsequent neglect in textbooks, is an early example of the "management" of history.[13]

The passion that is aroused by controversial treatment of certain historical events indicates how important historical myths are to a government, to a people, to a group, and how powerful a tool the use of history can be for "cultural aggression." Here I would like to refer to one recent example, described in *History Wars*—the Smithsonian Institution's proposed exhibition of the Enola Gay, along with historical commentary. The passionate response which this provoked seemed to reopen all the divisions in American society and the historians who contributed to the project were abused and attacked from every side. As Michael Kammen writes: "Historians become notably controversial when they do not perpetuate myths, when they do not transmit the received and conventional wisdom, when they challenge the comforting presence of a stabilized past."[14] The angry emotions aroused by the exhibition, the inability of Americans to agree on what had happened on August 6, 1945, show how unused Americans are to facing conflicting ideas about their own past. There is a preference for a history where ideals rather than realities triumph, where slavery, civil war and imperialism are seen as passing aberrations: "The holy nation thus acquired a holy history. A conspiracy of myth, history and chauvinism served to create an ideology as the dominating historical motif against which all history would resonate."[15]

Harmful enough to the people of a nation whose history is thus celebrated, the attempt to present a pleasing myth of the past is even more dangerous for the peoples of other regions and cultures. The spell may bind. The imperialist project made great use of its portrayal of a benevolent, progressive history in which the colonized could be integrated. Both France and Britain set up libraries in the Middle East and North Africa to perpetuate their own view of their history. Today's American project uses the American Cultural Centers to persuade others to identify with and internalize American values and policy goals. Control of material reduces the recipient's ability to judge, refute or contextualize.

In the following articles are an attempt at addressing some of the ways in which an image can be accepted as real and assimilated by an outside group or civilisation, sometimes to its own detriment. How attention is paid to packaging history, for ends that are known to the agent but unknown to its victim; the power of the image, a power often more potent than that of reality. The first essay, deals with the Chartists' passionate conviction that the Americans possessed a democratic system and that such a system would produce prosperity for all, despite certain known facts that contradicted this idealising vision, and their belief that the Americans were benevolent: "their sympathies travel across the Atlantic on behalf of the enslaved millions of the working classes in the Old World."[16] The suggestion is that the Chartists ignored certain values and institutions that existed in their own and other European societies to adopt without question the American stance on the corruption and injustice of the Old World, with the Chartists seemingly blind to the fate of Indians, Mexicans and Negroes. It seems that this attitude has been mirrored in the 20th century: people of the Third World tend to confuse the image presented by the West with reality, and fall between a longing for that which they can not have (unlike the Chartists, most of them cannot now emigrate to the Western countries), or an attempt to introduce into their own cultures assumptions and value systems which frequently destroy the cohesiveness of those very societies.

The second article offers a few examples of how education can be used to influence foreign perceptions of the U.S. both of its domestic history and of its relations with the outside world. Recognition of the psychological factors in foreign policy execution has led the USA to provide free material, and selected books, to foreign students in order to produce a body of American-trained government and private leaders, imbued with the traditional picture of U.S. history as progressive and benevolent. There is little public knowledge in America itself about the content of U.S. propaganda directed abroad and the machinery by which it is disseminated; it is therefore clear that foreigners, with their yet more limited access to data, should encounter problems in assessing and judging certain U.S. claims and prescriptions. I echo Edward Said's amazement at the collective Arab amnesia about the U.S.'s assault on Arab history and regimes, and comment on the PLO's acceptance of the American construct of history and policy goals and their consequent vulnerability.

The third article addresses the use made of victims; showing how certain victims—five dead in the Boston Massacre, for example—are more useful than others, and how without a powerful group to exploit their sufferings victims will receive little attention; also how their sufferings may be "hijacked" by that powerful group in the interests of its own agenda. I review various attempts by British 19th century politicians and writers to exploit the Bulgarian Horrors, while the victims were lost sight of. I note the status and hierarchy of victimhood and the iconic significance of numbers ("in Jewish Holocaust studies...the figures of six million Jews and five million 'other' victims of Nazi extermination have assumed a status of almost scriptural unassailability"[17]) and consider how some victims can eclipse others.

The fourth article considers how differently the British and the Americans responded to the possibilities of Jewish immigration into Palestine and the forming of a Jewish army, showing how their own historical constructs (as well as pressure of outside factors) determined their attitudes to the Zionist project and how, in the words of Richard Crossman, "America could have nothing but a Zionist policy in Palestine."[18]

Lastly, I look at the Palestinian *intifada* and the American Jewish response to this. How the mythical presentation of a demonic, potentially all-destructive Yasser Arafat and PLO gave way to a more nuanced and realistic assessment, eliciting some sympathy for the Palestinians and for a two-state solution. The Israeli lobby's in the U.S. response and proposing another Arab enemy (Saddam Hussein) and linking him with the PLO, and how the events of 1990/1991 dealt a blow to the Palestinians' hopes that various UN resolutions in their favour would be implemented and brought them into a peace process sponsored by an extremely pro-Israel U.S. administration. This peace process has so far brought little to the Palestinians, particularly in economic terms, while enabling the Israelis to continue settlement activity.

Three of these articles were presented at a series of seminars held in the University of Tunis on themes that explored the boundaries between East and West. Here great ambiguity was expressed regarding the West's attempt to impose its political and civilisational construct on a Muslim world—an attempt nicely illustrated by a Peace Corps worker who told the participants at one conference that America was there to help them into the modern world with all its attendant consumer goods. Some participants argued that an analysis of some of the ways in which the colonizing powers and the U.S. have affected the Middle East ran the risk of degenerating into polemics. This is possibly true. But if we remember Toynbee's line of argument, would it not be better for the West to consider the implications of its modernising policies, its promotion of free-market economics, its insistence on women's rights and the environment better for the Middle East and for itself? Can the West promote its own history and agenda while neglecting those of the region? Has the West considered *why* Saddam Hussein was (temporarily) so wildly popular among the people of the Third World?

To abandon cultural aggression and become familiar with the "Other's" history would be to renounce the monopolising of morality, the propagandist version of one's own history, and to accept the merits of a comparative outlook. It could be argued that this is easier for those who have lived long outside their country. I have lived and taught in North Africa for a quarter of a century and have also had fairly extensive contact with the PLO, as well as Americans and British. Having been lucky enough in 1985 to have moved out of my home near Hammam-Chott a few days before the resort was bombed by the Israelis, killing both Palestinians and Tunisians, I do have a degree of personal involvement. I admit to feeling strongly about the region's future choices. I am concerned when historical information which is of vital importance to those living there is withheld and when attractive versions of the past are offered in its place. But here I should like to commemorate the passion of Eric Hobsbawm, as shown in an interview given in October 1994. Asked whether his Marxist bias could infect his writing ("It needn't particularly..."), and whether all historians were to be found somewhere on a political spectrum, his reply was: "Yes. All serious ones. Unless you are simply a chronicler or compiler of dictionaries."[19] I would defend my own position by suggesting that for any historian there is at least the temptation, and perhaps the duty, to become polemical— "Historians are constantly challenging the received wisdom and established interpretations of events. *This is what they do.*"[20]

NOTES

1. P. Glazebrook, *Journey to Kars* (Harmondsworth: Penguin, 1985), p. 63.
2. A. Toynbee, *A Study of History* (London: OUP/Thames and Hudson, 1972), *passim*.
3. K. Marx, *Capital* (Moscow: Foreign Language Publishing House, 1961, English edition London: Lawrence and Wishart) vol. 1, p. 11.
4. Marx, *op. cit.*, p. 20.
5. A.L. Rowse, *The Use of History* (London: English Universities Press Ltd., 1946), p. 23.
6. *Idem*.
7. Rowse, *op. cit.*, p. 69.
8. Toynbee, *op. cit.*, p. 10.

9. H. Zinn, *A People's History of the United States* (London and New York: Longman, 1980), p. 570.

10. Zinn, p. 574.

11. Gwyn Prins, "Oral History," in P. Burke, ed., *New Perspectives on Historical Writing* (Cambridge: Polity Press, 1991), pp. 127, 128.

12. J. Lukacs, *Outgrowing Democracy: A History of the United States in the Twentieth Century* (New York: Doubleday & Company, 1984), p. 35, p. 397, note; M.S. Sherry, *In the Shadow of War: The United States since the 1930s* (New Haven and London: Yale University Press, 1995), p. 176. For a description of the situation in Texas, for example, see G.C. Edwards, "Texas, The Big Southwestern Specimen" in D.H. Borus, ed., *These United States: Portraits of America from the 1920s*, (Ithaca and London: Cornell University Press, 1992), pp. 352-3.

13. The Galloway Plan (by which a British Parliament and an American Parliament could mutually veto the other's legislation when affected by it) was defeated by a one-vote majority. All reference to this "was subsequently expunged from the records of Congress, however, and the plan is almost forgotten by American history." This was a "striking example" of "managed news." (R.A. East, *John Adams* (Boston: Twayne Publishers, 1979), p. 48, and p. 108, note 14, citing M. Jensen, *The Founding of a Nation: A History of the American Revolution 1763-1776*.)

14. Quoted by P. Boyer, "Whose History Is It Anyway? Memory, Politics, and Historical Scholarship," in E.T. Linenthal and T. Engelhardt, eds., *History Wars*, (New York: Henry Holt and Company, 1996), p. 131.

15. N. Huggins, quoted by M.B. Young, "Dangerous History: Vietnam and the 'Good War'," in *History Wars*, p. 200.

16. *Reynolds's Newspaper*, July 6, 1856.

17. J.W. Dower, "Three Narratives of Our Humanity," in *History Wars*, p. 79.

18. Hansard, vol. 460, col. 987.

19. Eric Hobsbawm, interviewed by Christian Tyler, "Post-mortem on a Bloody Century," *Financial Times*, October 15, 1994.

20. Boyer, *op. cit.*, p. 134; my italics.

THE REAL AND THE IDEAL: AMERICA AND THE CHARTIST DREAM

The inhabitants of the United States are governed on the principles of Chartism, the consequence of which is that all legislation is bent towards the welfare of the many.[1]

The Chartists (and they were not alone in this) saw in the United States a model of change for Britain: so much was shared by the two nations that America's speedy progress towards male democracy was viewed by critics as a dreadful warning, or by apologists as a promise, of what Britain could become.

Many British institutions and assumptions introduced by British colonists lived on in America after independence, among these a political structure which linked political power to possession of land. The Americans "democratized" their system much more speedily than the British. The "Jacksonian Era" in the U.S. coincided with the passing of the Reform Bill in Britain, and the further opening of the U.S. system to male suffrage and political democracy occurred at the same time as the Chartists were demanding these things in Britain.

In this essay I shall address the position of the Chartists, who had a vision of political democracy that was to a certain extent implemented in the U.S.; their basic argument was that empowering the people would lead to a better life, economically and morally. The Chartists' demands were pragmatic: reform was being advocated "that it might do us some good...not for the gratification of any abstract or metaphysical whims."[2] Political reform would change society. Their premise was that a better society existed in the U.S. and could be imitated in Britain. But their assessment of American democracy was faulty, and the economic and social conditions existing in the U.S. in the "age of the common man" did not justify their enthusiasm for that democracy. How then can we explain the extravagance of the hopes placed in the U.S.?

The Chartists' enthusiasm for the American system was unbounded, extravagant, illusory:

there we see millions of contented and happy human beings.... There we see a government which of necessity advances the happiness of the people because the whole people through their representatives have formed the government. [3]

Just as the Chartists idealized a mythical English past, so they posited an ideal America, ignoring the economic crises that beset that country, the real conditions of workers and farmers, and the fate of those not white, Anglo-Saxon and Protestant. They glorified the revolutionary period; G.J. Harney's letters reveal that "from my boyhood Boston has been to me as the Mecca or Jerusalem, and Faneuil Hall as the Caaba or Temple of modern Freedom"—Faneuil Hall being "the famous cradle of Liberty." In Washington he wrote: "Thousands of times I had longed to enter Independence Hall," and to him Virginia's soil was "sacred."[4] Uneasiness about slavery did not prevent him romanticizing the past; like many Chartists, he could not understand why the Civil war was not proclaimed a war against slavery, why the federal army was returning slaves to their masters, and why the 1862 election results in the northern states were so disappointing. Only Massachusetts preserved his ideal of "Freedom and free America."[5]

G.D. Lillibridge points out that for radicals "the migration of American democratic success to their own land was a fervent hope, a constant dream, and they were firmly convinced that the American example was to reshape and recondition their own lives and their own society."[6] The argument ran that American government was cheap[7] (they did not wonder at whose expense); and that the combination of universal suffrage and cheap land brought freedom; they denied palpable facts: "in America, riots never occurred"; and stated as a fact that full male suffrage existed.[8] The *London Despatch* wrote on 15 January 1837:

> In the United States, the eye of the traveller is gladdened by the sight of man's constantly increasing happiness, and his ears are hailed by the approbation of the many to the few who govern under the millions, chosen by the millions, acting for the millions, and responsible to the millions.[9]

The *English Chartist Circular* viewed America as a beacon: "the bright luminary of the western hemisphere whose radiance will extend across the Atlantic's broad expanse and light the whole world to freedom and happiness"[10] with E. Jones agreeing that "the mission of America is to liberate the world."[11] In 1856 *Reynolds's Weekly* proposed that America "must help to make enslaved states free and independent also."[12]

Adulation prompted the use of American discourse: in the 1840s, extracts from the *Working Man's Advocate*, *Young America*, *The Radical* and *The Daily Sentinel* appeared in *The Northern Star* and other Chartist papers.[13] Chartist Associations were named after iconic figures such as Washington. Prominence was given to the U.S. in public processions, and in the big procession to celebrate O'Connor's release from prison in 1841 a banner carried the slogan, "The Glorious Republic of America, and soon may England imitate that country; its people happy and contented."[14] There was even a proposal that America should intervene in British politics: after the 1839 uprising, Thomas Parkins urged the Chartists to send a memorial to the U.S. President to intercede with the British Government to have British people granted the same rights Americans enjoyed; though the suggestion was eventually rejected, after a tied vote, by the Council of the Metropolitan Charter Union on 7 June 1840, *The Southern Star* printed the memo along with approving letters.[15]

The Chartists' enthusiasm was based firstly on a misapprehension of the exact state of American democracy. They believed their demands were in force in the U.S.; to what extent was this true?

The first demand was: "A VOTE for every man twenty-one years of age, of sound mind, and not undergoing punishment for crime."[16] During the revolution, rich patriots seeking support against Britain lowered property requirements to involve unenfranchised Americans in their struggle. By the end of the 18th century some 60-90% had the vote, depending on where they lived.[17] In the first half of the 19th century the U.S. population rose from 4 million to 23 million (1790-1850)[18] and the electoral system became increasingly unrepresentative as population rise, industrial development and migration affected residence and population patterns and types. In both Britain and the U.S. there was a corresponding widening of the suffrage base. Since the U.S. Constitution allowed states to define their own political structures, there was a wide variation of voting requirements, and change happened sporadically. As various minority and property-less groups demanded the vote, what conservatives like James Kent in New York had termed the "idol of universal suffrage"—"an awful power"[19]—was increasingly introduced during the Chartist period, though many states retained tax-paying qualifications (South Carolina, from 1835; Pennsylvania, until 1877; New Hampshire [after the 1851 enquiry]; Rhode Island, until 1887; Massachusetts). Progress was uneven: white adult male suffrage was introduced gradually in the new Western states (Indiana, Illinois and Missouri), Mississippi (1831), New Jersey (1844), Connecticut (1844-5), Louisiana (1845), Ohio (1851) and Virginia (1851).[20] Often there was a hidden agenda to this widening of the franchise: in Louisiana white male suffrage was intended to unite all whites against Negroes, thus protecting "our state and its institutions against the diabolical machinations of abolitionism."[21]

For one group the suffrage was not being extended but was rather contracting. Free Negroes were being deprived of the right to vote, not only in the Southern states, such as North Carolina, where the free Negroes were disfranchised after 1835 (no free Negro or mulatto to the 4th degree inclusive could vote by 1839) but also in the North and Border states: in Maryland, where Negroes had voted, an 1810 amendment cancelled this right; in New York where 6,000 free Negroes had the vote in 1821, they had been disfranchised by 1846; in Delaware the 1852 Revised Statutes prevented them from voting or holding office. "By 1840 blacks had been disfranchised in the South, as well as in New Jersey, Pennsylvania and Connecticut, where they had once enjoyed the vote, and exercised political rights only in New York (providing they could meet property and residence requirements), Massachusetts, New Hampshire, Vermont and Maine."[22] Ninety-three percent of free Negroes in the North lived in states that excluded them from the franchise. By 1860, only 6% of free Negroes lived in the five states where they could still vote, and in only three of these did they have equal rights to whites as concerned voting. "Northern Negroes remained largely disfranchised, segregated, and economically oppressed."[23]

An English visitor to the free states, Captain Marryat, outlined a case where a Negro, James Forten, was unable to vote, though extremely rich (a usual qualification for suffrage), and quoted a Supreme Court decision: "Men of colour are destitute of title to the elective franchise."[24]

It was not that Negroes were backward in their demand for the vote: from the 1830s, black conventions had sent petitions to federal and state governments to ask for the suffrage (and for equal legal and educational rights), and from the 1820s seventeen black newspapers called for their rights.[25]

Women were equally disfranchised. The advance of democracy had deprived women of a former power: to wield power as queen, consort, relative, mistress. Now parliaments and assemblies were all-male bodies, voted for by men alone. As industrial capitalism promoted the idea of the male worker and male rights, women were left outside the political process. After the American Revolution, none of the state constitutions except that of New Jersey gave women the vote, and New Jersey rescinded this right in 1807.[26]

For local elections, the voting qualification was usually stricter than for state or federal elections. Vermont and the new Western states had tax-paying qualifications (for example Louisville, Kentucky; Ashport and Memphis, Tennessee; St. Louis, Missouri; Vincennes and Jacksonville, Indiana; Chicago, Illinois).

Even where the suffrage was extended, various devices were used to skew election results. Residence requirements excluded the extremely mobile poor (in ante-bellum Boston, for example, the total turnover in a decade could reach several times the city's total population).[27] Elections were held at times which favoured the rich: harvest-time (Virginia, Louisiana) but not in September in New Orleans when yellow fever voided the town of well-to-do. Sunset laws were used to disfranchise labourers. Registration also reduced the voting electorate. All in all, the percentage of voters was higher than in Britain: Heale estimates that in the 1840s, with similar populations, 2.4 million Americans voted in presidential elections, whereas under 1 million British men were qualified to vote.[28] But this was not the Chartists' universal male suffrage.

Indeed, the Chartists could have noticed events happening at that very time in Rhode Island which presented a number of similarities to their own struggle, as, indeed, leaders there were aware. In Rhode Island, where non-voters were excluded from juries and courts, only 4 out of 10 adult white males could vote; they were told to buy land if they wanted to vote, but land was becoming scarce and industrial workers' wages were low. In quickly-growing Providence, freemen constituted only 16% of the town's 21,000 residents. (Also there was great inequality in representation, with the rural south controlling the urban north.)[29] In 1841 the Rhode Island Suffrage Association, using language and concepts that could have been written by Chartists[30] encouraged delegates to elect a Popular Convention and that Convention to write a Constitution ending property qualifications for the suffrage. In the May 1842 elections two rival governments were elected; the old governor and legislature started arresting all those who held office under the People's Constitution and fomented ethnic and religious passion—it was argued that the new Constitution would place all the state's institutions "under the control of the POPE of ROME, through the medium of thousands of NATURALIZED FOREIGN CATHOLICS."[31] Governor Thomas Dorr, with 234 men, attacked the arsenal, martial law was declared, $1,000 was offered for Dorr's capture, 300 people were arrested, and a new, compromise, Constitution was issued. The vote was given to freeholders with one year's residence or property-less Americans with various qualifications for various types of seat.[32] The old property qualification remained for naturalized foreigners. Negroes, who had joined the fighting against Dorr, were given the vote. A strange result was that where 15,000 had voted in the 1843 elections, by 1850 only 4,000 voted—20% of the population—just like Britain!

As in the case of the demand for universal male suffrage, the Chartists' other claims were partially, gradually and sporadically implemented. Instead of a secret ballot, there was either open voting, for example "straight arm," where voters were marched to the polling place with their coloured ballots, distributed by the parties, visibly in evidence; otherwise, stuffed ballot boxes and counterfeited ballots permitted fairly wide-ranging corruption. As for the abolition of the property qualification for Members of Parliament, amendments in New Hampshire in 1852 removed the property qualification for Representatives, Senators and the Governor, but generally speaking property requirements remained and the legislators were rich men. Regarding payment of M.P.s, Marryat commented in 1839 that in Congress Representatives and Senators were paid; however, states differed in the amounts paid.

Nor was the Chartist demand for equal constituencies perfectly implemented. Self-interest ensured that politicians elected in existing districts were unwilling to change boundaries to reflect shifts of population to the towns; districts were frequently drawn to give the maximum advantage to the already dominant party. As for elections to the House of Representatives, in 1842, state legislatures were directed to subdivide their polities into congressional election districts each of which would send one representative to the House. Again, constituencies were contrived for partisan advantage. As most state legislatures were controlled by rural legislators, districts were designed to give rural areas greater representation than cities. For example, in Rhode Island before 1841 the rotten boroughs left the urban population underrepresented in the lower house; in South Carolina, although the upcountry, with 4/5ths of the white population, controlled the lower house, the upper house was dominated by the low country, with 1/5th of the white population but 4/5ths of the state's wealth. This lasted until late in the century. The Chartists' demand for annual elections was more nearly approached: although each state could fix the periods of elections, New York had annual elections to its House of Assembly; South Carolina too; and in Congress, Representatives were elected biennially.

* * * *

Despite this partial democratization, there was widespread poverty, acute in times of depression. "Hardship and deprivation were for many people becoming as normal as comfort and hope."[33] The grand crises of 1837 (where 200,000 out of a total New York City population of 500,000 were in "hopeless distress")[34] and 1857 were separated by minor crises, and there was even reverse migration (18,814 returned to Britain in 1858, and 17,798 in 1860).[35] In 1839 farmers in Albany, New York, hit by depression, were unable to pay rent or debts. Bank collapses brought ruin in their train, as in Baltimore, where the Bank of Maryland collapsed. Slums existed (in Philadelphia in the Jackson Era working class families lived fifty-five to a tenement with no garbage removal, no toilets, no fresh water; in New York the poor lay in streets, there were no sewers) and bred disease: there were epidemics of cholera (1832), typhoid (1837) and typhus (1842). Conditions were bad, not only in the industrial towns of the north, but for the vast poor white population of the south; a North Carolina paper in 1855 spoke of "hundreds of thousands of working class families existing upon half-starvation from year to year."[36] F.L. Olmstead emphasised low living standards and ignorance; no southern state had a public school system, and many people received no schooling at all; "the majority of free white men lagged far behind other civilized societies in education, material standards, and economic opportunity."[37]

By mid-19th, "the legal system had been reshaped to the advantage of men of commerce and industry at the expense of farmers, workers, consumers, and other less powerful groups within the society...it actively promoted a legal redistribution of wealth against the weaker groups in the society."[38] Discriminatory tax laws, laws for private incorporation that helped the businessmen at the expense of the working class, rent laws helping landlords against tenants, conspiracy laws helping employers against unions were all examples of class legislation. English common law was set aside: judgments for damages against businessmen were heard before judges, not juries; the idea of a just price was replaced by that of purchaser's responsibility. Individualism triumphed; there was no sense of community; few charitable institutions existed; "legislative protection for women and children in industry...was achieved more rapidly in England than in America"[39] and "public welfare hardly existed."[40]

Mob action was a frequent response to such misery. There were the Baltimore riots of 1835 (when the bank collapsed), the New York Flour Riot of 1837, the Kensington, Philadelphia, Protestant-Catholic riots in 1844, the 1849 New York Astor Place anti-actor and anti-Irish riot, the "beer riots" of the 1840s and 1850s, the 1857 Newark, New Jersey unemployment riot, the New York draft riots of 1863, plus anti-Mormon and anti-abolitionist riots. In 1834 there were 16 riots and 37 in 1835; between 1829-1850 there were five major anti-black riots in Philadelphia alone.[41] The U.S. was also the land of slavery. Frederick Douglass ridiculed America's "great principles of political freedom and natural justice": "Go where you may, search where you will, roam through all the monarchies and despotisms of the Old World, travel through South America...and you will say with me that, for revolting barbarity and shameless hypocrisy, America reigns without a rival."[42] Whereas slavery had been outlawed under the "reactionary" laws of Britain the U.S. Congress refused even to discuss the question.[43] The 1807 law against slave importation was not enforced and perhaps 250,000 slaves were illegally imported into the U.S. before the Civil War. Nor did the U.S. support the treaty to control the slave trade. The British Navy was not allowed to search American slavers, "with the result that most of the slave ships, in the 1850s, not only flew the American flag but were owned by American citizens."[44] There were frequent calls from the South to reopen the African, and expand interstate, slave trade. Between 1850-60, 80,000 Negroes were exported from the Border States to the South.

There was also violent racism in the Northern states, especially, as de Tocqueville had remarked, in states where slavery had never existed. Parts of the U.S. were to be Negro-free: pioneers in Oregon and California adopted restrictive measures in the late 1840s to prevent Negroes going West. In the Free States Negroes suffered from segregation and economic oppression and were denied most civil rights; severe laws were passed to prevent them moving there. In general, Negroes, whether free or slave, were seen as a danger to the very existence of the U.S. Mobs attacked Negroes and abolitionists: in Boston, in 1830 David Walker was assassinated; in New York, in 1834, black churches were burned; in Boston, in 1835, "the mob rose in triumphant brutality to murder George Thompson" and "thirsty for blood, demanded Garrison"[45]; in 1839 Negroes were attacked in Cincinnati[46]; the 1863 New York draft riots saw "every black man marked out for murder...beaten to a jelly, hanged on lamp posts.... Houses set on fire for the gratification of burning Negro men alive."[47] Their civil status was low; according to Thomas R. Dew, among "Massachusetts prison inmates blacks represented a proportion 12 times higher than could be justified in terms of their numerical presence in the state. Everywhere they belonged to the very lowest orders of society."[48]

This was also a period of intensive land appropriation. In 1844, only 30,000 of the 120,000 Indians living east of the Mississippi in 1820 still remained (as a result of attacks on Indian culture, disruption of Indian food supplies, and a whole range of collective punishments as well as a policy of forced expulsion). Under President Jackson, 94 treaties were passed in 8 years to appropriate millions of acres of Indian land. The 1830 Indian Removal Act empowered the President to exchange Indian land in the east for areas in the Great American Desert; removal treaties were signed with tiny minorities, migration was enforced by the Army, and the federal government then failed to provide its promised aid and protection to the migrants.

As for the Mexicans, first Texas and then half of their remaining territory was taken by the U.S.; although the 1848 treaty guaranteed Mexican rights, they were seen as racially inferior and suffered much discrimination, many landowners being dispossessed in the 1850s, while the federal government failed to protect them.

When considering the Chartists' enthusiasm for their American ideal, it seems to me that two separate issues emerge. The Chartists were presenting class-based demands, elaborating links between economic problems and political representation: had American "democracy" improved conditions for the working man? The other issue is, were the Chartists interested in a wider liberty, or were they restricted by their rhetoric of resistance to crown, aristocracy and middle class oppression so that they failed to recognise Negroes, Indians or Mexicans as fellow sufferers?

The first issue addresses the existence in the "democratic" U.S. of a wretchedness that the Chartist programme had been devised to prevent. The Chartists were not alone in their delusions about political democracy; in America the "contrasts between the ideal of a more perfect society and the realities of actual existence were always apparent, but they became of special significance when every speech and every newspaper proclaimed that the road to earthly paradise lay over American soil."[49]

The Chartist writer J.F. Bray, who had lived in the U.S. and still communicated with family there, explained in a witty book (9/10ths of which was devoted to criticism of Britain) how democracy and wretchedness could coexist: at elections "[t]he struggle is generally between a greater and a lesser aristoc, and on the side of each are arrayed both aristocs and commos...duped to become the tools of the aristocs." Propaganda is used:

> [The wealthy] loudly proclaim that themselves and the commos are equal in every respect—that no man has the right to ride upon the back of another—that to do so is an act of flagrant and unendurable tyranny.... Yet, notwithstanding all this outcry—made simply to amuse the commos, and keep them in love with their political plaything, which allows them to choose aristoc governors only—the aristocs of Amrico ride the unfortunate commos without mercy.

He points out the hypocrisy involved: "With all this accumulated mass of black and white slavery, the Amricos boast perpetually of their freedom and enlightenment."[50] He was rare among Chartists to see so clearly.

Despite the rhetoric, power did not go to the common man. P.H. Burch explains: "The nature of the federal recruitment pattern will have a profound effect on the government's policy-making process and thus, almost inevitably, on the distribution of benefits in society."[51] He describes how the 1 to 2% of the population who constituted a strategic elite (occupying major cabinet, executive and diplomatic positions) ruled from the Jackson era to the 1853-7 Pierce administration. While the rhetoric flattered the common man, power was really in the hands of lawyers, plantation owners, entrepreneurs, bankers, land speculators and railroad directors. Under Jackson, "about 95 percent of the people to hold high appointive office during this period were elite figures."[52] Also, in the 1840s and 1850s, 73% of cabinet, diplomatic and Supreme Court officials had had a college education and 95% had elite socio-economic ties, with railroad contacts increasingly important.

This explains why the situation of factory workers, labourers and the poor worsened in the "era of the common man" and why the railroads, for example, enjoyed big land grants from the government at every level. Indeed, in 1850-7 the railroads used their political contacts (Senators A. Douglas, L. Cass and T.H. Benton) to get 25 million acres of public land almost free (and provided a free transportation service for Douglas's 1858 campaign!) The New York Central Railroad was said to run the Democrat Party there; from the 1840s the Camden and Amboy Railroad controlled governors and legislators; and generally links between politicians and railroad interests were strong.

And in the cities, too, a rich elite ruled, despite a tax-paying suffrage. E. Pessen describes four cities (and extrapolates for other towns):

> Ante-bellum governments were governed largely by the propertied for the propertied.... Municipal budgets were minuscule, largely because wealthy tax-payers were known to be unwilling. Wealth was notoriously under-assessed because rich men insisted it be.... Social inequities and pervasive misery were not simply dealt with in a niggardly way; they were treated as the wages of sin and of individual fault.

Politics were dominated by the wealthy, who ensured that local government would reflect their interests. Pessen concludes that "the common man had little influence, let alone power, in the nation's cities during the era named in his honor."[53] The result of this was an increasingly inequitable distribution of wealth; by 1845, 4% of New York City's population owned 66% of the property, and in 1860, 1% of Philadelphia's population possessed 50% of the wealth.[54]

A wide use of propaganda helped Americans to forget reality. The English traveller E.S. Abdy noticed how Americans thought they were "the greatest people under the canopy of heaven" because they were told it so often in "fourth of July orations, in sermons, and speeches, and reviews, and magazines, and newspapers..."; and Americans were encouraged to view Europe as barbarously backward.[55] Additionally, bribery and corruption were rife and the two-party system was exploited to defuse class anger and prevent working class solidarity. Parties headed by rich men blamed scapegoats (racial, religious, political) for bad conditions. By 1840 both parties' leaders were "socially indistinguishable from their opponents"[56] and there were "organizational, ideological and membership similarities between the two dominant parties."[57] Workers' parties could not stand against the big mainstream parties; by 1834, the mechanics' and working men's parties that had been formed in 1828-30 in New York, Pennsylvania, New Jersey and New England were dead, split by ideological strife, personality conflicts and the slander and infiltration of the main parties.

Was it that the Chartists were ill-informed about the realities of the American political and social situation; or were they merely reluctant to admit that their programme had failed?

The flow of individuals and information back and forth across the Atlantic ensured that current events were well reported in either country: President Van Buren was well informed on the 1832 Reform Bill and the Dorr rebels on Chartism, while Parliamentary debates referred to American events such as the 1837 Panic. But the Parliamentary reports *also* accepted as given that the U.S. was a country of universal suffrage (Lord John Russell: "There they have universal suffrage") and the ballot; their argument was merely that these did not guarantee prosperity, and that the U.S., like Britain, suffered from corruption, crises, distress, forged bank notes etc. The unwelcome argument that *no form of suffrage* could "ensure lasting prosperity to the people" could be dismissed as class-based, coming from a body which had refused to even consider Chartist petitions.[58]

Distinct from the hard facts of political reporting was the American rhetoric that even its victims adopted. Free Negroes, disfranchised in most states, still used the official discourse in their conventions, expressing "their admiration for the Declaration of Independence, their gratitude for having been born in a bountiful land, and their faith in 'the spirit of American liberty' "[59]; when suffering Negroes could internalize this idealised image, or at least use its rhetoric, how could the Chartists, reading extracts from the U.S. press printed in Chartist papers, doubt their ideal, particularly when it was what they wished to believe?

Anecdotal information came from visitors returning from the U.S., and these were legion—Methodists who had attended General

Conferences, failed emigrants, and wealthy travellers. Many of these complained about the *style* of American society and politics—the venality and violence of elections, "men on the make, frontier primitivism, crass materialism, defiantly non-deferential manners, national self-assertion and Anglophobia"[60] but this would be seen as class prejudice, along with the Methodists' distaste for the "despotism of pure democracy."[61] Charles Dickens, who had intended to correct earlier travellers' impressions, who had "dreamed by day and night, for years, of setting foot upon this shore, and breathing this pure air" found that "this is not the republic of my imagination.... In everything of which it has made a boast...it sinks immeasurably below the level I had placed it upon; and England, even England, bad and faulty as the old land is, and miserable as millions of her people are, rises in comparison." Dickens—with such a wide readership, no wonder he was a disappointment to the Chartists—reported on the "[p]overty, wretchedness and vice" in New York's Five Points area and the terrible conditions in prisons and insane asylums generally; he issued a vituperative attack on the hypocrisy of the politicians in the Capitol who protected the institution of slavery while in the same city was displayed the Declaration that "All Men are created Equal." In the Congressmen he saw:

> the wheels that move the meanest perversion of virtuous Political Machinery that the worst tools ever wrought. Despicable trickery at elections; under-handed tamperings with public officers; cowardly attacks upon opponents....[62]

Captain Hall's and Captain Marryat's criticisms[63] might well be discounted by Chartists because of their class source. But what about J. Bray: "There are no greater tyrants in existence than the moneyed republicans of the United States" in a land where "they, like ourselves, are divided into rich and poor—into capitalists and producers—and the last are there, as they are here, at the mercy of the first"[64]; or the Radical T. Brothers, who returned to Britain after years spent in labour politics and agitation for the 10-hour day to tell of the bribery, false returns and casting of illegal votes: "Those that attend the votes are become so corrupt and selfish, that they anxiously look for these annual bribes as their daily bread." He wrote to the Chartists citing an American trade unionist's letter: "'Tis true that once a-year they call us men, freemen, intelligent, virtuous, orderly, working men, but then they want our votes" and describing the man's situation—elected to the House and then betraying his class: "his wages as a member saved him from starvation, and the sale of his votes finally procured him an independence." Or Allan Pinkerton: "most Chartists in coming to this country [who] are willing to sell there love of Equal rights for the Smiles & Crumbs of the So Called Democratic Party."[65]

A number of Chartists went to the U.S. Although the accidental and fragmentary nature of the material prevents us getting a complete picture of these émigrés, R. Boston compiled a list of 70 Chartist émigrés, and further information is found in D. Thompson's *The Chartists* and other Chartist literature.[66] Boston reckons that between 1839-60 some 500-600 Chartists went to the U.S., of whom one-third returned to Britain, often disgusted and proclaiming themselves Tories! "Physical force" Chartists who fled Britain after the Newport rising and the Plug Riots, and whom Boston thinks constituted half of the returnees, usually returned very quickly. They migrated to avoid arrest or after prison; it seems that in 1840-1 H. M. Inspector of Prisons, Major W.J. Williams, offered all Chartist prisoners in 1840-1 free travel to the U.S.[67] "Moral force" Chartists tended to stay longer, and some crossed and re-crossed the Atlantic. Their complaints usually addressed the corruption and hypocrisy of the American political system and the difficulty of finding employment. John Alexander, in the U.S. in 1848-9, bewailed its "hopeless condition as regards either moral, political or intellectual progression"; Thomas Ainge Devyr poured scorn on American politicians: "'Democrats...?' They call themselves Democrats, but they are all thieves."[68]

And yet the Chartists continued to promote America and encourage emigration there. Although there were reports of bad economic conditions there was continuing information on sailings to the U.S., boarding houses (sometimes run by Chartists), tips on where to go, and lectures, letters from emigrants, and accounts of American life. In the 1848-9 number of *The People*, a letter from an America returnee warned against encouraging emigration, and Barker's reply is most illuminating. He said he had never encouraged people to look for work in Boston, New York, Philadelphia or any of the seaboard states: migrants "should hasten at once into the *interior of the country*, and never stop *at all* till they have got as far as OHIO"; this is backed with another letter in which a correspondent "recommends his friends to emigrate to America, and not to stop till they reach Ohio or Illinois."⁶⁹ This is both a recognition that life in the big cities was no better than in Britain, and something very interesting—that the Chartists were going for reasons other than the liberty which they extolled: for cheap land, not for the rights of the Indians, the Mexicans and the Negroes.

* * * *

The Chartists' "liberty" excluded the native Americans; rather they idealised the man who perhaps despoiled them most—Andrew Jackson, "land speculator...slave trader, and the most aggressive enemy of the Indians in early American history." From Jackson's 1814 treaty (as treaty commissioner) with the Creeks, and the 1814-24 treaties, and the 94 treaties signed under his administration, from his military campaign into Florida, and his Indian Removal Act, "the leading measure" of his administration and consequent expulsion of Choctaws and Cherokees, Jackson's stance was clear.⁷⁰ Yet he was acclaimed at Chartist meetings, "honored with radical toasts, his biography widely advertised, and on his death was given the full treatment as a hero of the common people."⁷¹ The Chartists were not concerned about the original owners of the land but about its destination. O'Connor argued that democracy in the U.S. depended on the success of the free land movement; Devyr linked American freedom with absence of landlords: "So long as land can be easily purchased by the in-coming emigrant, all shall go well"; and O'Brien stated that free land was the only hope for world democracy!⁷² Vincent reported on his return from the U.S. how he had met a former Chartist shoe-maker, starving in Britain: "Here he is a farmer with 160 acres of good land; his wife in cosy comfort with him, and seven children all doing well."⁷³

Nor did the Chartists pay much attention to the Mexicans. Visitors generally were affected by the Manifest Destiny syndrome and the idea of vast spaces being developed by British stock, clearly stated by J.G. Bennett: "all other races...must bow and fade" before "the great work of subjugation and conquest to be achieved by the Anglo-Saxon race,"⁷⁴ and the Chartists were no exception, calling for the annexing of Texas and Mexico, and some even fighting in the U.S. Army against Mexico.⁷⁵ Now the Mexican Constitution made slavery illegal, while it was legitimate under the U.S. Constitution, and Calhoun stated clearly that the U.S. was annexing Texas *to stop*

Britain abolishing slavery there, because this could harm the institution of slavery in the U.S.[76] How seriously can we take the Chartists' interest in liberty? As Edward Said has noted, an alien hegemony is equally oppressive whether its source is liberal, monarchical or revolutionary.[77]

In their enthusiasm for America the Chartists supported various American attempts to take parts of Canada from their "British oppressors,"[78] proclaiming that America's mission was to liberate the world. But Negroes in the U.S. knew Canada as one terminus of the Underground Railroad, or asked to be sent there rather than be handled by Colonization Societies. Which "liberty" was being protected against which tyranny?

This leads us to talk again about slavery. Travellers returning to Britain marvelled at how the discourse of freedom could exist alongside the institution of slavery. Dickens was shocked that it was defended "as if it were one of the greatest blessings of mankind" and devoted an entire chapter of *American Notes* to a passionate attack on American attitudes to Negroes and American Indians.[79] H. Tudor believed that "as long as slavery is allowed…America must forgo its proud claim to superior advantage over the rest of mankind." E.S. Abdy pointed out that there were over 70 capital crimes for Negro slaves and only 2 for whites: "So much for liberty in America."[80] De Tocqueville himself saw slavery as the greatest of America's defects, and the introduction of slavery into new states as "a crime against the human race."[81] But the Chartists' stance was ambiguous, and many criticized abolitionists for opposing the 10-hour movement or for addressing black claims before the white men had been "freed."[82] Chartists did not emigrate to the Southern states, they later said they had not considered these as part of the U.S. (a strange excision of half the nation and misreading of the U.S. Constitution)![83] Hundreds (thousands according to Harney) of Chartists emigrated. Most of them went to the North or West; and many took up farming, or organising white workers. They seem to have been unsympathetic to problems outside their own class experience; a sort of selective, Eurocentric blindness operated.

M.C. Finn argues (in another context) that their rhetorical strategy "limited the ability of radicals to endorse novel political ends—notably property redistribution" and that their constant attribution of the evils of the age to corrupt, repressive state institutions "impeded radicals' willingness to elaborate or entertain sustained critiques of industrial expansion."[84] It also prevented them addressing the problems of other races; they thought as white Anglo-Saxon males; the enemies they identified were class enemies; despite their internationalist and liberty-loving discourse, the solutions they sought were in their own interests.

The most important questions are: does political democracy with all its ritualised tools and platforms necessarily ensure economic and social happiness? And does democracy result in ethical policies? Thomas Brothers put this dilemma succinctly: "It is held, by all modern democratic writers, that where universal suffrage and election by ballot are established, there good government must exist as a matter of course."[85] He then raged against the Americans' treatment of Indians, Negroes and Mexicans. Alexis de Tocqueville, formerly an admirer of American democracy, deplored the Kansas-Nebraska fighting, the extension of slavery, the fighting with Mexico, the prospect of war with Cuba, and more generally "that spirit of conquest, indeed of rapine, which you have been displaying for several years"[86]; his correspondent Jared Sparks argued that democracy and conquest were in fact *linked*:

> a spirit of adventure and conquest excites the aspirations and moves the will of the people. Perhaps it is inherent in the democratic element. The clamor for acquiring Cuba springs from the same spirit; and a slight cause would carry the arms of the United States again into Mexico.[87]

(To develop this idea I would like to cite a 20th century source: a paragraph from a U.S. State Department Record of a meeting of the State-Defense Policy Review Group meeting on 16 March 1950: "there are very few things that a democracy cannot do if given a particular combination of circumstances and necessity. It is impossible to draw a sharp line between democratic principles and immoral actions, and an attempt to do so constitutes a dangerous and unnecessary handicap."[88])

There has been an attempt to show that the application in the United States of Chartist principles (partial only) did not produce general prosperity but racism and conquest. Did the Chartists not know? Or did they not care? The first question is easily answered: there was significant debate both in Britain and in the U.S., and the English working class was well informed through their own press and via individual correspondence—even a power-loom weaver like

"John Ward" living in Clitheroe knew in a most sophisticated manner about all the ins and outs of the Civil War.[89] But did they care? It is hard to explain the absence of attacks on the Americans' faults, and the constant support for emigration and lauding of American liberty and prosperity, other than by a mind-set which preferred image to reality and land to liberty. They did know. And they did not care.

NOTES

1. *The Charter*, Oct. 20. 1839, quoted in F. Thistlethwaite, *The Anglo-American Connection in the Early Nineteenth Century* (Philadelphia: University of Philadelphia Press, 1959), p. 43.
2. W. Cobbett, *Political Register*, 22 June 1833, quoted in J.T. Ward, ed., *Popular Movements c. 1830-1850*, (London: Macmillan Press, 1970), p. 51
3. *The Weekly Chronicle*, March 12, 1837, quoted in G.D. Lillibridge, *Beacon of Freedom: The Impact of American Democracy upon Great Britain 1830-1870* (Philadelphia: University of Pennsylvania Press, 1954), p. 31. *Reynolds's Newspaper* of July 6, 1856, stated: "they are blest with institutions a thousand years in advance of ours."
4. *The Harney Papers*, ed. F.G. Black and R.M. Black, Van Gorcum & Comp. (Netherlands: N.V., Assen, 1969), pp. 111, 154, 157, 165.
5. *Idem*, p. 111. On December 10, 1862, Harney found the elections in New York and other northern states most disappointing. The belief that the Civil War was fought to eradicate slavery was one held by many Chartists. However, his disappointment did not prevent him going to the U.S. the following year.
6. Lillibridge, 4-5.
7. This debate involved Chartists and politicians; politicians in Britain pointed out that it was America's almost unlimited acres that enabled her to have cheap government. *The Poor Man's Guardian* of June 30, 1832, reported MP Henry Hunt: "America—there we find a republican government, and there we also see a government that is cheap." (Lillibridge, p.15).
8. H. Hunt, see Lillibridge p.33.
9. *The London Dispatch*, Jan. 15, 1837, quoted in Lillibridge, p. 42.
10. English Chartist Circular, Feb. 13, 1841, quoted in Lillibridge, p. 40.
11. E. Jones, *People's Paper*, Sept. 4, 1852, in Lillibridge, p. 83. The *People's Paper* had a circulation of c. 3-4,000. America aimed not only at mere expansion but "at a nobler field of victory: moral conquest of liberty, the subversion of tyranny" in the old world as in the new. (*People's Paper*, Sept. 3, 1853)
12. *Reynolds's Weekly* (c. 100,000 circulation), quoted in Lillibridge, p. 84.
13. Thistlethwaite, p. 67.
14. M. Hovell, *The Chartist Movement* (Manchester: Manchester University Press, 1918; reprinted 1970), p. 226.
15. Lillibridge, pp. 43-4 and Thistlethwaite, p. 62. The suggestion, made after the 1839-40 risings, that the President should intercede for Chartists was rejected at the 7 June 1840 Council of the Metropolitan Charter Union; the circulation of *The Southern Star* was c. 2,000.
16. All quotes from the Charter are as published in the *Socialist Standard*, January 1982.
17. M. Mann, *The Sources of Social Power* (Cambridge: Cambridge University Press, 1993), vol. II: *The Rise of Classes and Nation-States, 1760-1914*, p. 153.

18. E.J. Hobsbawm, *The Age of Revolution 1789-1848* (New York: The New American Library, 1962), p. 204.

19. James Kent was speaking against the abandoning of the property qualification at the 1821 New York Constitutional Convention, reported in J. MacGregor Burns, *The American Experiment: The Vineyard of Liberty* (New Delhi: Swarn Printing Press, 1986), p. 364; P.N. Carroll and D.W. Noble, *The Free and the Unfree: A New History of the United States* (Harmondsworth: Penguin Books, 1977), p. 197.

20. C. Williamson, *American Suffrage from Property to Democracy 1760-1860* (Princeton: Princeton University Press, 1960), p. 266.

21. Williamson, p. 266, citing the *Journal of the Proceedings* (of the 1845 Convention), New Orleans, 1845.

22. A. Barbrook and C. Bolt, *Power and Protest in American Life* (Oxford: Martin Robertson, 1980), p. 66.

23. C. Van Woodward, *The Future of the Past* (Oxford: Oxford University Press, 1989), p. 270.

24. Captain F. Marryat, *Diary in America (1837-8)* (London: Longman, Orme, Brown, Green & Longmans, 1839; reproduced London: Nicholas Vane, 1960), p. 177. James Forten was extremely rich (he possessed about $150,000) and, though a taxpayer, could not vote; p. 184. Marryat had stood for Parliament unsuccessfully in 1833. He wrote his diary to "examine and ascertain *what were the effects of a democratic form of government and climate upon a people which...may still be considered to be English.*" (p. 46). The Americans disliked his diary, calling it "coarse vituperation."

25. Barbrook and Bolt, pp. 65-67 describe the efforts of 60,000 free Negroes to get equal suffrage, legal and educational rights, and an end to segregation.

26. H. Zinn, *A People's History of the United States* (London: Longman, 1980), p. 109.

27. M.J. Heale, *The Making of American Politics 1750-1850* (London: Longman, 1977), p. 208.

28. Williamson describes the various ways in which voters were excluded from the polls; on p. 283 he remarks of the 1840s: "Probably, in any state, the smallest increase in the size of the electorate was about 10 percent and the greatest increase about 50 percent...confusing an increase at this time in voter participation with the separate phenomenon of increased enfranchisement, critics believed that men of substance and education were being swamped at the polls by newly qualified voters." The comparative figures for Britain and the U.S. are given by Heale, p. 223.

29. G.M. Dennison, *The Dorr War: Republicanism on Trial, 1831-1861* (Lexington: University Press of Kentucky, 1976), pp. 26-7.

30. Dennison describes how the Rhode island Suffrage Union adopted a charter, declared the right of all free citizens to participate in government, and decided to petition the General Assembly and if need be Congress; it founded local chapters and ran a newspaper, the New Age. It faced the identical problem the Chartists had—what to do if the petition was refused. Zinn, pp. 209-211 also describes the Dorr rebellion.

31. Scare tactics used in "Native American Citizens! Read and Take Warning," 1842, quoted in P.T. Conley, *Democracy in Decline: Rhode Island's Constitutional Development 1776-1841* (Providence: Rhode Island Historical Society, 1977), p. 321.

32. Conley, Zinn and Williamson all give details.

33. J.R. Pole's 1980 lecture, "American Individualism and the Promise of Progress" (Oxford: Clarendon Press, 1980), p. 24. Pole remarks that the connection between self-seeking individualism and competition was becoming clear after the 1837 crash. Parke Godwin called in 1844 for a system like Fourier's to be used against laissez faire capitalism and the "monopoly of the great capitalists" (p. 25).

34. Zinn, p. 220. That year in New York one-third of the working class had no work.

35. R. Boston, *British Chartists in America 1839-1900* (Manchester: Manchester University Press, 1971), p. 81.

36. Zinn, p. 231. Zinn describes the millions of poor whites in the South, cultivating land so poor the plantation owners had abandoned it. The Federal Census of 1850 showed that one thousand Southern families received about $50 million a year, while all the other families, some 660,000, received about $60 million a year. H.R. Helper in *The Impending Crisis of the South: How to Meet It* (New York 1857; new ed. Cambridge, Mass.: Harvard University Press, 1968.) believed that only with the ending of slavery would the poor whites' conditions improve, in a modernised, industrial South, from which all Negroes had been expelled.

37. F.L. Olmstead, *The Cotton Kingdom* (New York, 1861; new ed. A.M. Schlesinger, New York: A.A. Knopf, 1953), used materials collected in 1852-3. Quoted in W.R. Brock, *Conflict and Transformation: The United States, 1844-1877*, *The Pelican History of the United States*, vol. 3, (Harmondsworth: Penguin, 1973), p. 137. Brock describes how despite a wide suffrage the elite had social advantage and economic power and blamed poverty, backwardness and lack of progress on external enemies; p. 85.

38. Zinn, p. 235, quoting M. Horwitz, *The Transformation of American Law, 1780-1860* (Cambridge, Mass.: Harvard University Press, 1977).

39. L.S. Marshall, "The English and American Industrial City of the Nineteenth Century," in D. Englander, ed., *Britain and America: Studies in Comparative History, 1760-1970* (New Haven: Yale University Press, 1997), p. 106.

40. Brock, p. 100.

41. L. Dinnerstein, R.L. Nichols, D.M. Reimers, *Natives and Strangers: Blacks, Indians, and Immigrants in America* (New York: Oxford University Press, 1990), pp. 118-120.

42. Douglass's 4 July 1852 Independence Day Address, quoted in Zinn, p. 178. For the slave, "your celebration is a sham; your boasted liberty an unholy license; your national greatness, swelling vanity; your sounds of rejoicing are empty and heartless; your denunciation of tyrants, brass-fronted impudence; your shouts of liberty and equality, hollow mockery; your prayers and hymns, your sermons and thanksgivings, with all your religious parade and solemnity, are to him mere bombast, fraud, deception, impiety and hypocrisy."

43. The slave trade was abolished in 1806 in certain British colonies; in 1807 the importing of slaves into any British colony was forbidden, as well as the carrying of slaves in British ships; in 1833 slavery was abolished in the British West Indies, Canada, Mauritius and the Cape of Good Hope. J.F. Bray, in *A Voyage From Utopia To Several Unknown Regions of the World, 1842,* (reprinted London: Lawrence and Wishart Ltd., 1957) pointed out that in the U.S., Congress had "done all in their power to render the wrong eternal, by forbidding all future discussion whatever upon the subject" (p. 147).

44. Zinn, p. 168, citing J.H. Franklin, *From Slavery to Freedom* (New York: A.A. Knopf, 1974). Franklin (1961 ed., p.182) shows that between 1854-60 every Southern commercial convention gave consideration to the proposal to reopen the slave trade officially; "for all practical purposes, the trade was open in the last decade before the Civil War." S.A. Douglas believed that more slaves were brought into the U.S. in 1859 than in any year when the trade was legal. N. Chomsky, *Year 501: The Conquest Continues* (London: Verso, 1993), p. 21.

45. *The Harney Papers*, p. 165. Harney was reminiscing in 1863 and could not remember whether this had happened in 1833 or 1835! Thompson was a British abolitionist, and W.L. Garrison the famous abolitionist who called the Constitution "an agreement with Hell." He was a friend of Harney's, and tried to get him a job when he resigned from the Jersey Independent in 1862 because of the editor's prosecessionist stance. Harney was also a friend of the abolitionist Wendell Phillips.

46. Dinnerstein, on various types of riot, describes the attacks on Negroes and burnings of black churches, and attacks on abolitionists, pp. 118-120.
47. Harney, p. 161.
48. H. Temperley, "American Society After Emancipation," in B.H. Reid and J. White, eds., *American Studies: Essays in Honour of Marcus Cunliffe* (London: Macmillan, 1991), p. 74.
49. Brock, p. 100.
50. Bray, p. 150, p. 143, pp. 147-8.
51. P.H. Burch, *Elites in American History*, vol. 1: *The Federalist Years to the Civil War* (New York: Holms & Meier, 1981), p. 27. For members of each administration Burch shows elite status, family status, occupational status, land-owning status, shareholder status, business connections, etc.
52. Burch, p. 159.
53. E. Pessen, *Riches, Class and Power Before the Civil War* (Lexington: D. C. Heath and Company, 1973), pp. 292, 299. Pessen tests the accuracy of the assumption that the rich had no political power in the U.S. by considering the wealth and standing of officeholders in New York City, Brooklyn, Philadelphia and Boston and the policies of these cities' governments; he also compares the political patterns of the big northeastern cities with other parts of the U.S.
54. Burch, p. 218 note 21, cites Pessen as showing how inequality, already marked in the Jackson era, had worsened considerably by the 1860s. In the South, 7% of the population owned 75% of the slave property.
55. E.S. Abdy, *Journal of a Residence and Tour in the United States of North America, from April, 1833, to October, 1834* (London, 1835), ii: 337, quoted in Heale, p. 195. Also, Dinnerstein (p. 115-6) quotes a Norwegian immigrant: "Three fourths of the people in the East and ninety-nine hundredths of the people in the West are fully convinced that the other side of the Atlantic is nothing but a heap of medieval feudal states" living in misery and anarchy.
56. Brock, p. 50.
57. Barbrook and Bolt, p. 39.
58. Sir Robert Peel in 1842 spoke of Britain having 150 years of "greater liberty and happiness than had been enjoyed by any other country, not excepting the United States of America" (Hovell, p. 257-8). Lord John Russell pointed out in the 1839 debate in Parliament that in the U.S. universal suffrage coexisted with economic distress, even though there was unlimited land (Hansard 3, 49: pp. 238, 263, July 12, 1839; and Disraeli warned in 1848 against the American experiment (Hansard 3, 99: p. 953, June 20, 1848). Benjamin Disraeli could have been considered a friend: he stood as a Radical candidate in 1832; he was one of only 3 to vote against a bill advancing money for the Birmingham police when there was a Chartist Convention there; and he was one of only 5 to oppose harsh sentences on Chartist leaders; "Nobody can deny that the Chartists labour under great grievances," he stated (quoted by M. Foot, *Debts of Honour* [London: Pan Books, 1980], p. 51).
59. "Declaration of Sentiment" of the Fifth Annual Convention for the Improvement of the Free People of Colour in the United States, meeting in Philadelphia in June 1835, quoted in Barbrook and Bolt, p. 67.
60. P.J. Parish, "'Political Arrangements, Social Absurdities and Wondrous Contrivances': British Men of Letters on Nineteenth-Century America," in Reid and White, p. 108.
61. L. Billington, "'To America We Will Go': British Methodist Preachers in the United States, 1800-60," in Reid and White, p. 49.
62. Charles Dickens, writing from Baltimore to Macready, quoted in E. Johnson, *Charles Dickens: His Tragedy and Triumph* (London: Penguin, 1986), p. 223. C. Dickens, *American Notes and Pictures from Italy* (reprinted London: J.M. Dent and Sons Ltd., 1931), pp. 87, 118-119.

63. Captain Basil Hall, *Travels in North America in the Years 1827 and 1828* (Edinburgh: Cadell & Co., 1829), criticised the lack of experience among politicians in a system which "neither brings the most qualified men into power, nor retains them long" (p. 278) and makes them into mere agents of the popular will; Captain Marryat after a one-year trip criticised the drunkenness, the levelling spirit, the mob violence and the racism in the Free States ("Is not this extraordinary in a land which professes universal liberty, equality and the rights of man?" p. 176) Both men were of a very different social class from the Chartists.

64. J.F. Bray, *Labour's Wrongs and Labour's Remedy; or, The Age of Might and the Age of Right* (Leeds: D. Green, 1839), pp. 20, 19. But Bray emigrated to the U.S. in 1842.

65. T. Brothers, *The United States of America As They Are; Not as they are Generally Described: Being a Cure for Radicalism* (London: Longman, Orme, Brown, Green & Longmans, 1840), pp. 136, 226. Brothers had emigrated to the U.S. in 1825 and turned to labour politics, taking part in 1835 in the agitation for the 10-hour day; he was in contact with Philadelphia labour leaders and New York radicals. He returned to Britain in 1839 to publish this book as a sad warning. In 1850, the same criticism was made by Allan Pinkerton (quoted in Black and Black, eds. *The Harney Papers*, p. 66), writing to Harney from Illinois, May 11. Pinkerton emigrated in 1842 and founded a strike-breaking detective agency.

66. Boston; D. Thompson, *The Chartists: Popular Politics in the Industrial Revolution* (New York: Pantheon Books, 1984); Hovell; Ward; Thistlethwaite; Lillibridge; J. Burnett, ed., *Useful Toil: Autobiographies of Working People from the 1820s to the 1920s* (London: Allen Lane, 1974); and the various Chartist newspapers.

67. Thompson, p. 220. Some of those who fled were: J. Astin (1848), twice arrested; P. Bussey (1839), implicated in the Newport rising, to avoid arrest; W. Butterworth (1842), after being jailed for promoting rebellion; J. Campbell (1843) "hurriedly"; G. Chatterton (1839) to escape arrest; W. David (1839); T.A. Devyr (1840) wanted after the 1839 violence in Newport when he awaited the signal; G.J. Holyoake (1848) after being in jail 1841-3; P.M. McDouall (did he go in 1853? or did he go to Australia and die?) after 1839 jail; R. Mellor (1839) in a hurry; J. Mitchell (1842) a wanted man; A. Pinkerton (1842) in a hurry; J. Rees (1839) after Newport, with 100 on his head; J. Rewcastle (1840) fleeing; W. Thornton (1839) wanted; J. Wolstenholme (1839) fleeing. The list is not definitive.

68. John Alexander, who stayed two months; quoted by J.T. Ward, *Chartism* (London: B.T. Batsford Ltd., 1973), p. 238; Thomas Ainge Devyr, Ward, *Chartism*, p. 240. Other Chartists returned to Britain: Feargus O'Connor, Lawrence Pitkeithley, Peter Bussey, William S. Brown, William Ashton (Ward, pp. 230, 238); William Aitken, James Astin, Joseph Barker (but he went back again in 1865), William Brown, James Dawson Burn, William Butterworth, William Carpenter, George Chatterton, Abram Duncan, John Fraser, George Julian Harney, George Jacob Holyoake, William Rider, Samuel Roberts, Henry Vincent, George White, John Wolstenholme, Benjamin Worswick (Boston, pp. 88-97); Richard Pilling (Thompson, p. 318).

69. *The People*, ed. Joseph Barker, Series I, vol. 2, pp. 13, 120. *The People* published accounts of Barker's visit to the U.S., advertisements for Emigration Societies, letters from America, times of sailings. It admitted that at the time there were thousands of tailors out of work.

70. Zinn, pp. 125, 129.

71. Lillibridge, p. 42.

72. Lillibridge, p. 70, O'Connor wrote articles in *The Northern Star* on these lines, 1844-45. Thistlethwaite, p. 65, quotes Devyr and describes his fight in the Antirent movement in Rensselaer County.

73. Thompson, p. 186. Henry Vincent reminisces about "French of Banbury."

74. T.R. Hietala, *Manifest Design: Anxious Aggrandizement in Late Jacksonian America* (Ithaca and London: Cornell University Press, 1985), p. 170, quoting J.G.

Bennett, editor, *The New York Herald*, 4 July 1845. *The Herald* was the largest selling paper in the U.S. in the 1840s, thus representative in its views. Also C. Mulvey, *Anglo-American Landscapes—A Study of Nineteenth-Century Anglo-American Travel Literature* (Cambridge: Cambridge University Press, 1983), p. 231. Both Mulvey and J.M. Woods, "In the Eye of the Beholder: Slavery in the Travel Accounts of the Old South, 1790-1860," in *Southern Studies: An Interdisciplinary Journal of the South*, New Series vol. 1 no. 1, Spring 1990, give a number of examples of travel literature. Alexander Mackay, *The Western World; or, Travels in the United States: Exhibiting Them in Their Latest Development, Social, Political, and Industrial* (London: J. Murray, 1849) believed that trivial faults like corruption should not hide the importance of the vast destiny awaiting the Mississippi region—"the chief theatre for Anglo-Saxon enterprise, and will yet witness the greatest triumphs of Anglo-Saxon energy and skill." Mulvey cites other writers, like Sir Charles Lyell, *Travels in North America: With Geological Observations on the United States, Canada, and Nova Scotia* (London: J. Murray, 1845), who also shared this exciting sense of Manifest Destiny.

    75. Boston, p. 81, gives M.M. Trumbull's words: "Of course, I knew nothing at the time of the ethics or the politics of the war with Mexico." Trumbull, who been out of work in the U.S., enlisted in the Army in Mexico in 1847, and again in 1860. Lillibridge, p. 63, shows the Chartists approving the peaceful acquisition of Texas (*Northern Star*, April 18 1846) but denouncing the violence used to expand into Mexico.

    76. Heale, p. 197. Calhoun wrote in 1844 to the British Minister in Washington. N. Chomsky, p. 27, describes U.S. fears that an independent Texas might be manipulated by Britain to abolish slavery in the U.S. Hietala, pp. 51-54, also stresses this idea.

    77. Edward Said, "Yeats and Decolonization" in T. Eagleton, F. Jameson and Edward Said, eds., *Nationalism, Colonialism and Literature* (Minneapolis: University of Minnesota Press, 1990).

    78. *The People*, ed. J. Barker, (vol. II, no. 71) printed p. 152 an extract from an American newspaper, *The People*, urging Americans to "prepare, if necessary, to fight in behalf of the Canadians against their British oppressors" (1850). Lillibridge cites the *London Dispatch*, March 12 and April 30, 1837 as urging Canadians to seek independence as a republic; and the *Weekly Dispatch*, January 2, 1842, stating that Canada south of the St. Lawrence should be given to the U.S.

    79. Johnson, p. 222; Dickens, *American Notes*, pp. 225-241.

    80. Woods, quoting Henry Tudor, *Narrative of a Tour of North America: Comprising Mexico, the Mines of Real Del Monte, the United States, and the British Colonies, With an Excursion to the Island of Cuba, in a Series of Letters Written in the Years 1831,1832* (London: J. Duncan 1834) p. 33, and Edward Abdy, *Journal of a Residence and Tour in the United States of America, From April 1833 to October 1834* (London: J. Murray, 1835) p. 34. Many others are cited as critics of slavery: Alexander Mackay (mentioned above), Harriet Martineau, *Society in America* (London: J. Saunders 1837), James Stuart, *Three Years in North America* (Edinburgh: Robot Cadel, 1833), James Silk Buckingham, *The Slave States of America* (London: Fisher & Sons, 1842), Rev. G.W. Featherstonhaugh, F.R.S. (the geologist) *Excursion Through the Slaves States, From Washington on the Potomac to the Frontier of Mexico: With Sketches of Popular Manners and Geological Notices* (London: J. Murray 1844). All these made known their dislike of the cruelty, family separations, forced marches, interstate slave trade and the American South's intolerance of criticism. But books would be expensive for Chartists to read.

    81. H. Brogan, "Alexis de Tocqueville and the Coming of the American Civil War," in Reid and White, p. 96, quotes a letter from de Tocqueville to E.V. Childe of 2 April 1857: "to introduce it into the new states, to spread this horrible plague over a large part of the earth's surface which has hitherto been preserved from it...is a crime against the human race, and to me seems appalling and inexcusable." This is echoed

on p. 92 in de Tocqueville's letter to T. Sedwick of 10 January 1857, "It would seem to me to be one of the greatest crimes that men could commit against the general cause of humanity."

82. The anti-abolitionist John Campbell, in the U.S. 1843-74: *Negro Mania: Being an Examination of the Falsely Assumed Equality of the Various Races of Men* (Philadelphia, 1851), accused abolitionists of opposing the 10-hour day, and T.A. Devyr, in the U.S. from 1840 til his death, who wished to see the white man freed first and became a Democrat politician.

83. Lillibridge, p. 118. "Was it reasonable to hope that *a section where the few governed the many...a community in which all power was absorbed by a few territorial lords* should hold its own against an entire nation of freemen, where every man possessed the suffrage and could exert an influence upon his government?" (my italics). They argued that the South was a hangover from colonial times!

84. M.C. Finn, *After Chartism: Class and Nation in English Radical Politics, 1848-1874* (Cambridge: CUP, 1993), p. 57, pp. 320-321.

85. Brothers, editorial. He had emigrated in 1825, where he published *The Radical Reformer*, and had contact with Philadelphia labour leaders and New York radicals but returned to Britain in 1839.

86. Brogan, in Reid and White, p. 86.

87. H.B. Adams, "Jared Sparks and Alexis de Tocqueville," in *John Hopkins University Studies in Historical and Political Science*, ed. H.B. Adams (Baltimore: John Hopkins Press, December 1898), quotes Sparks's letter to de Tocqueville of June 13, 1853, commenting on the acquisitions of Texas and California. pp. 45-6; in this vol. Pp. 607-8.

88. M. Curtis, *The Ambiguities of Power: British Foreign Policy since 1945* (London: Zed Books Ltd., 1995), p. 18.

Burnett, pp. 77-89, gives extracts from the diary of John Ward (identified as John O'Neil) for the years 1861-in which the writer talks about prospects of war between Britain and the U.S., prospects for emancipation of slaves, the 1864 presidential elections and their implications for the pursuance of the war, the Chicago convention's nomination of an opponent to Lincoln, the war commander and Democrat General McClellan, and Lincoln's triumph.

ACROSS BOUNDARIES: WHERE HISTORICAL CONSTRUCT MEETS POLITICAL ACTION

This study was written as a consequence of reading rather startling comments from my Arab students which betrayed a growing sympathy for the U.S. version of its history and a growing identification with the Americans themselves and a correspondingly uncritical attitude to the U.S.'s current policy goals.

They believe that the early settlers fled from religious persecution and sought religious freedom in the new land; they note British tyranny while ignoring the colonists' massacres of Indians and the harsh exploitation of indentured servants; they express shock at the Boston massacre (3 shot dead, 2 died later) but ignore the larger numbers killed by local elites crushing levelling riots. I give a sample of student comments from recent papers: "They wanted to build a whole democratic life," "They were courageous and full of hope." The Declaration of Independence was a "commitment to... greater social and economic equality"; "The new government based on equality came at the head of their claims." "They were poorly equipped but their courage pushed them to struggle in order to survive"; "They were courageous enough to overcome all the difficulties." The heroic picture surprises. Would our students have written thus about other white settlers) the South Africans? The pieds noirs? The Israelis?

Our students seem to see the Americans as innocent victims—of religious persecution, of political repression, of a corrupt world they must relinquish isolation to repair. They seem to accept the concept of American exceptionalism, that America has a unique, God-given role to play to improve the human condition and that it is unlike any other country—altruistic, righteous, passive rather than aggressive. For someone of my generation this is unexpected. It shows me that perhaps the decades of anti-imperialist suspicion of the U.S. and U.S. motives have perhaps passed. That people of a developing country should be led by attractive packaging of history and current events to identify with Americans and internalise their values and policy goals is most dangerous; that a certain construct of U.S. history and portrayal of the U.S.'s role on the world stage should be used to change other nations' own value systems and interests, is alarming.

Edward Said in his book *Orientalism*[1] shows how cultural domination is maintained and proposes that the Arab world is an intellectual, political and cultural satellite of the U.S. He pays specific attention to the situation in the universities, where lack of books and research facilities combine to prevent Arab students gaining access to modern or alternative material. A conference held in Tunis in September 1991 decided that Arab researchers should not have too many illusions about freedom of academic thought, facing the constraints of financial pressure, media neglect, discrimination as to being published, etc. The situation is made worse by the ever-present, pervasive influence of the cultural milieu, with its attendant consumerism, and the insidious attack on academic excellence by programmes such as "Saved by the Bell," where fun and sex are shown as more desirable than study.

So it is important that students approach with care the literature made available to them. Foreign currency requirements have meant that most new books are out of the question for students and thus libraries constitute the major source of information. The American Cultural Center (which I recognise does provide a range of literature, although many critical works are absent) provides certain books free of charge, and it is these books—easily obtained by students—that I shall use to illustrate some of my arguments. These are: *An Outline of American History* (produced by the U.S. Information Agency), the *Family Encyclopedia of American History* (published by the Reader's Digest Association, Inc.), *An Early American Reader* (the U.S. Information Agency), and *About the United States* (again the USIA), plus *Forum magazine*, which is produced by the U.S. Government Printing Office and distributed by U.S. embassies abroad, plus *Wireless File*, available at the U.S. Cultural Center.

The USIA was formed in 1953-4 to tell America's story to the world because traditional agencies failed to pay sufficient attention to the "psychological factors in foreign policy execution." "Communication designed to win support—or at least acceptance (of policies)—is present at every U.S. Embassy." Books and pamphlets provide the "weapons of the Free World" for a "psychological warfare attack" (the words of the Democrat and Republican Parties in 1964).[2]

This attack targets schools and universities and presents a glowing version of U.S. history as that of "a nation born of the idea of individual freedom tempered by respect for the freedom and rights of others." It relays the "idea of freedom and the principles on which America is based" to help "people in other nations engaged in building democratic governments and free-market economies."[3]

As well as providing literature, the USIA operates an exchange-of-persons programme for students, teachers, researchers and experts: "The United States produces abroad a body of American-trained government and private leaders...benefits to the United States in both the short and the long range are generally great," a sympathetic USIA staff member writes approvingly.[4]

The importance of propaganda is increasingly recognised. FBI Director William Webster (though he was referring to hostile elements) said groups which "produce propaganda, disinformation and 'legal assistance' may be even more dangerous than those who actually throw the bombs."[5] We should pay heed to this statement.

Interestingly, we read in Tunisia what neither Americans nor British people can read. "Americans are insulated from their own national information apparatus by a congressional policy designed to protect them from being propagandized by their own government," the USIA man continues. The "content of United States propaganda abroad and the machinery by which it is disseminated" is kept from the American public.[6] While in Britain I attempted to procure some of the books I mentioned above. Neither town or university libraries stocked them. The U.S. Embassy refused to reply. It is equally impossible to be subjected to U.S. propaganda in the U.S. and Britain; it is the Third World the books are designed to inform. Their purpose is therefore clear.

I shall now take four popular student misconceptions and show how these books encourage a certain vision of U.S. history.

Let us start with the idea that the Puritans emigrated to flee persecution. We should bear in mind the context of the large-scale 16th and 17th century European persecutions and the fact that the Anglican church was designed under Elizabeth precisely to avoid this danger. It was to be a national church that embraced the majority of the people and included both Catholic and Protestant elements in dogma and ritual. Elizabeth, stating that she intended to open no windows into men's souls, insisted on a minimum outward compliance only. But the Puritans wished to impose their minority wishes on the majority; their dispute with Elizabeth continued into the next century and when they saw under Laud the Catholic element being stressed they realised they were losing ground. The concept of a national church was anathema to them: they believed any form of Catholic practise ("Popish trash" as William Bradford termed it) had to be rooted out, and they believed that only the elect, the saved, and not the majority of the people (or the ruler) could be church members. Tolerance and moderation were to them the enemies of obedience to God's will, to the covenant with God; in Britain, they had under the Protectorate expelled Anglican clergy and punished incorrect belief. They felt themselves obliged to set up a theocracy, to stamp out unconformity, to institute the kind of regime Calvin had set up in Geneva, in short, to emigrate. It was not persecution they fled, but God's anger.

Leaving aside the fact that hunger for land was the major motive for emigration (advertisements from shipping companies and proprietors all offer land as the attraction, and none that I have seen mention religion), and that many emigrants left Britain involuntarily (prostitutes, criminals), even the original Puritans did not migrate for religious reasons alone. The Pilgrim Fathers saw in Holland that few would join them because of the "hardness of the place and the country" and that more material attractions were necessary to tempt Puritans to leave Britain. If the religious motive was not sufficient to tempt people to Protestant, Indian-free Holland, a much more pressing motive must have sent them to Indian-infested America. And even on the famed Mayflower, only 35 of the 102 passengers were Puritans. The rest were not travelling for religious reasons.

Our students think the Puritans believed in religious freedom. But once in America, the religious elite governed church and colony; only the saved could vote; exile or death awaited those with different beliefs; the Blue Laws imposed Biblical norms with severe punishments; and the ideal community was perpetuated with each new settlement. Such strict control over every aspect of life led finally to events like the Salem witchcraft trials. Nathaniel Hawthorne's story *Young Goodman Brown* conveys the sense of schizophrenic alienation, with all citizens in positions of social trust discovered to be in league with the devil.

The Puritans' intolerance extended to the Indians, whom they slaughtered, seeing themselves as modern Israelites and the Indians as a modern Amalek.

In our books, the Puritans are shown as wishing to "reform" or "purge" the Anglican church with "simpler forms of faith and worship"; it is implied that they could not practise their religion freely and were "resisted at every turn." The Anglican attempt to merge Catholic and Protestant doctrine is derided as "the typically English compromise of a Book of Prayer." Puritans migrated to avoid "persecution," being barred from university appointments. Only one case of a colonist's being forced into exile is given, and a social and political, not religious, reason is offered. The Salem executions are described as done "in a final outburst of misguided zeal." An "important step in the direction of democracy" was taken when officials were elected in public meetings: "Since that time, Americans have viewed their country as a great experiment, a worthy model, for other nations."

Our students' second misconception is that the Americans were a colonised people suffering under tyranny and that, like all colonised people, they longed for freedom. In fact, the 1775 Declaration of Causes and Necessity of Taking Up Arms stated that the Congress did not mean to "dissolve that union which has so long and happily subsisted between us, and which we sincerely wish to see restored"[7] and that it had no intention of establishing independent states.

These were colonisers and Englishmen, with the rights and privileges of Englishmen living in England. This was constantly stated by British and colonists alike. As expatriates, they were subject to the same king and laws as their fellows back home; they enjoyed greater latitude, because further from the centre, but were expected to obey Parliamentary law on imperial matters. They were, as PM Pitt said, the sons and not the bastards of Britain. Newspapers such as *The Boston Advertiser* in 1749 suggested that they were luckier than their compatriots back in Britain, enjoying all the British rights plus additional ones. From the 1606 Virginia Charter onwards they insisted that they were "to have and enjoy all Liberties, Franchises and Immunities...to all Intents and Purposes as if they had been abiding or born, within this our Realm of England."[8] All charters insisted on this, right up to the 1772 Boston Town Meeting. They were asking for their "birthright as Englishmen."[9]

By the 1740s, governors complained that British laws were being flouted and that not a shadow of respect for the mother country remained. Distance and deceit made colonial trade regulations unenforceable; the colonists industrialised and smuggled. The colonies jealously guarded their place in the imperial system but refused to observe the regulations as regarded other colonies or Britain. Britain, after failing to prevent colonial expansion in 1763, suggested that the colonies contribute to the Army's expenses since a greater area had to be defended. The colonists refused to provide men or money, even the small sums Britain proposed, which would have obliged a colonist to pay one-fiftieth of what a British taxpayer contributed. One is reminded of the French colons in Algeria, or the Zionists in Mandate Palestine, protected by the mother country but angry when interests diverged.

This in the context in which the Boston Tea Party should be seen; colonists complained about taxation without representation while turning down British suggestions that their representation in Parliament should be augmented. Many allowed that Parliament could tax them for imperial matters.

Our books ignore the complex nuances of rights and types of representation; they ignore the fact that taxed tea was being sold in most colonies and that it was the arrival of cheaper taxed tea—undercutting smugglers' profits—that aroused ire. They do not mention the fact that the richest merchants were omitted from the list of consignees and had a personal interest in preventing tea imports and squeezing out small merchants. They talk of "taxation without representation"; say the Tea Act was passed to help the British East India Company; and say the "patriots" "persuaded" merchants who sold the tea to resign, when in fact torture was used. They ignore the temporary and coercive nature of the 1774 Acts and present these as an attempt to "punish Boston." They do not mention the Peace Commission with its offer of pardons and its abandoning of any attempt to get compensation paid for the tea.

One of the richest smugglers and politicians was John Hancock, with over 500 smuggling convictions. He was not on the list of consignees. He was one of the two men to whom Britain refused a pardon. *Forum* portrays him thus: "John Hancock was a wealthy New Englander who was president of the Continental Congress, nine times governor of Massachusetts, and a signer of the Declaration of Independence. The story goes that when he sat down to sign the Declaration of Independence, he remarked that he would write his signature so large that King George could read it without his spectacles."[10]

A third student error is to view America as destined to become the U.S. (A land for a people, as the Israelites, and Golda Meir, viewed Palestine.) This sense of bonding of land and people is proposed in *Forum*, January 1993, with a poem by Robert Frost:

> "The land was ours before we were the land's
> She was our land more than a hundred years
> Before we were her people."
>
> There was "salvation in surrender...
> (The deed of gift was many deeds of war)
> To the land vaguely realising westward,
> But still unstoried, artless, unenhanced."

Capture gives legitimacy.

The teleological sense that America could only become the U.S. sets the U.S. apart from other nations and ignores the fact that for a long time America was a prey to every kind of colonising activity and that changes there were a by-product of what was happening in Europe. U.S. history books, even the more radical, rarely offer this sense of being on the sideline of world events. But the War of Independence was won because it was part of a European war, and the young nation was hemmed about by colonial possessions which changed hands as a result of European power struggles. The U.S. learned to play the Europeans off against each other and to play a waiting game (Jefferson advised accepting Spanish rule in the south and west until "our population can be sufficiently advanced to gain it from them piece by piece."[11])

When European fighting died down, the Monroe Doctrine was issued to keep European powers out of the hemisphere while allowing the U.S. to interfere. Promoting republics, necessarily weaker than the empires, gave the U.S. weak states on its borders which could then be invaded. As Simón Bolívar, El Libertador, said in 1822: "There is at the head of this great continent a very powerful country, very rich, very warlike, and capable of anything."[12] Americans migrated into Mexico and when its constitution did not protect slave property rebelled, founding the state of Texas. Annexing Texas would give the U.S. command over the world cotton market (the 19th century equivalent of oil) and place all nations at the its feet. The U.S. annexed Texas and later invaded Mexico, of which it obtained the greater part.

As Frederick Douglass wrote in *The North Star* on 21 January 1848, "Mexico seems a doomed victim to Anglo-Saxon cupidity and love of dominion."[13]

Our books paint a less aggressive picture. "The vision of liberty had stirred the people of Latin America from the time the British colonies had gained their freedom," and the Monroe Doctrine was a response to threats to "lands which had freed themselves from their former overlords." The "acquisition of Texas" is presented in terms of domestic politics alone: should it join the U.S., being a slave-owning state? It "naturally entered the Union as a slave state." Thousands of Americans had "found Mexican rule increasingly oppressive" (taxation, cutting off of immigration) and rebelled with a "small, skilled army." "Texans didn't want independence; they wanted their land to be part of the United States." Then, "some Americans talked about taking over all of Mexico. But for $18-1/4 million the boundary was set along the Rio Grande." (The figure was derisory compared to federal profits from the sale of Indian lands.) Mexico was invaded because "Mexico still claimed an area of Texas north of the Rio Grande." Little attention is paid to any Mexican claim. As Walt Whitman said: "What has miserable, inefficient Mexico...to do with the great mission of peopling the New World with a noble race."[14]

For my last example I take the Marshall Plan. Months after World War II ended, the U.S. prepared for war with the USSR and secretly arranged for atomic weapons to be stationed in Britain. Britain would not be consulted, or necessarily informed, on their use. The Moscow Conference, starting in March 1947, was sabotaged by the announcement of the Truman Doctrine, which split the world into two blocs and forced every nation to choose between them, introducing an ideological crusade against oppression and terror. When the Conference (understandably) failed, State Secretary Marshall instructed the Policy Planning Staff to prepare a plan for the reconstruction of Europe, bypassing the existing UN Economic Commission for Europe, which included the eastern bloc. The Soviets, who had waited three years in vain for a U.S. loan, were told they would be expected to integrate into Europe as the agricultural, dependent, element, and would, George Kennan believed, be asked to divert resources from their own economy to aid Western Europe. He thought the Soviets would be subjected to U.S. pressure until they either broke up or changed their approach. State Secretary Dean Acheson said he aimed to "establish a flourishing Western community that would serve as a magnet to the Kremlin's eastern satellites,"[15] dazzling the satellites with Western prosperity.

Aid would be given to states wishing to preserve their democratic institutions against internal or external Communist pressure and would stop if a country voted the Communists into power. This was an incitement to Communist countries to leave the USSR and an interference in the internal affairs of states such as France or Italy, where indigenous Communist parties might have been elected.

It also corresponded to the U.S.'s export needs by closing the dollar gap. It permitted the penetration of imperial markets and opened up Europe. Transnational companies prospered on orders "fuelled initially by the dollars of the Marshall Plan."[16] Acheson admitted that the $16 billion was "only in part suggested by humanitarianism" and was "chiefly a matter of self-interest."[17]

Our students' books present the Plan more altruistically. Europe is described as "ripe for the extension of Communist influence" and unable to revive on its own; the U.S. decided "to ease Europe's plight." The U.S. offered aid to all countries; "The Soviet-bloc nations denounced the Marshall Plan but the Western Europeans enthusiastically welcomed it." With U.S. aid, "the results were spectacular. Europe knew unprecedented prosperity and a new economic unity." Jean Monnet is cited as saying, "The world has been a better place because of this."

So we return to the idea of American exceptionalism. Generations of U.S. writers, thinkers and politicians have seen America's cause as being that of all mankind. The U.S. is seen as a second but unfallen Eden. Herman Melville wrote that with the U.S. "for the first time in the history of the earth, national selfishness is unbounded philanthropy; for we can not do a good to America but we give alms to the world."[18] Politicians were viewed as extraordinary beings and icons were made out of political events. (Cf. the painting of George Washington by an unknown Chinese artist, from an engraving by Simon Chaudron and J.J. Barrelet, Henry Francis du Pont Winterthur Museum).

This sense of the exceptional nature of the U.S. is instilled in American students, but others do not need to accept it.

Politicians such as Ronald Reagan proposed that the U.S. is exceptional. "America is less of a place than an idea...nothing but the inherent love of freedom in each one of us..... God in shedding his grace on this country has always in this divine scheme of things kept an eye on our land and guided it as a promised land." The Founding Fathers were not normal figures but that "little band of men so advanced beyond their time that the world has never seen their like since." (No wonder our students talk of demi-gods!) Reagan invented a new version of the signing of the Declaration of Independence: "There stood up a man and spoke out and with his voice all was stilled. He said, 'Sign that document, sign it if tomorrow your heads roll from the headman's axe'." When they tried to find this inspiring figure, the "doors were guarded, and they asked the guards and no one had seen anyone leave; and no one knows to this day although his words are recorded, who that man was nor could they find anyone who had spoken the words that caused the Declaration of Independence to be signed."[19] The Biblical cadences and mention of a magical figure from another world lift history to myth.

Our students' books also promote a mythical, triumphalist, personified version of history, where the Declaration of Independence "set forth a philosophy of human freedom thenceforth to be a dynamic force in the entire western world." Where Abraham Lincoln, referred to by Wendell Phillips as "that slave-hound from Illinois"[20] is said to have "long regarded slavery as an evil." Where Reagan "backed democratic forces in El Salvador" and Carter "stunned many diplomats by announcing that U.S. relations with other countries would be based on a concern for the rights of humans."

An interesting mirror image in present in the world today. As the U.S. presents a certain historical construct and a set of policy goals to the world, so does Israel present a historical construct and set of policy goals to the U.S. As the U.S. pays attention to targeting colleges and universities to disseminate information, so does Israel pay special attention to targeting American colleges and academic institutions. Israel's version of history and current events certainly influences the U.S., and this then affects us. Just as Americans are occasionally alerted to the purposes of Israel's propaganda, so should we be aware of the purposes of U.S. propaganda, since it reflects not only U.S. but also Israeli interests.

Paul Findley recounts how AIPAC, the Israeli lobby, recognises the crucial role of American schools and universities for moulding opinion and disseminating propaganda. He describes the tactics AIPAC uses to control and monitor information: enemies lists, intimidation, returning Arab gifts to their donors (e.g. the Khashoggi grant to finance Arab-U.S. understanding).[21] AIPAC also liaises with over 200 campuses in its Political Leadership Programme, and uses programmes to recuperate black sympathy. For example, in January 1993 the Israeli Government and the United Negro College Fund jointly paid for presidents of seven black colleges to visit Israel and learn in Israeli universities that "politics is not everything."[22] AIPAC also acts to prevent research on topics such as the Holocaust.

Not only universities are targeted but also decision-makers: AIPAC offers free-of-charge history and news to Congressmen through the *Near East Report*. Arab or American attempts to present the Arab case are foiled, as Findley and also C.E. Edwards show.[23] Arabs are accused of dominating the U.S. media, and though the preponderance of Jewish journalists makes this extremely improbable it is suggested that Americans are subjected to massive Arab propaganda. Thus, magazines such as *Flame* set out to "counter incessant and sophisticated anti-Israel and anti-Semitic propaganda by the Arabs and the native bigots." In the same way that the *Near East Report* presents "myths and facts" about Israel, so *Flame* rewrites history and asks such questions as why "the Arab countries and the 'West Bank' should be the only places in the whole wide world where Jews are not allowed to live?"[24]

Attention is paid to promoting a historical construct which resembles that of the U.S. Formerly Americans noticed similarities between American and Israelite history; now the Israelis point out parallels between U.S. and Israeli history. When the Anglo-American Committee was visiting Mandate Palestine, the Zionists were advised by Judge Felix Frankfurter to take American Committee members to the new settlements and show them new-born children in a conscious attempt to remind them of the Far West pioneers. Parallels were drawn between Zionist settlers and Americans, Palestinians and aboriginals. This mirror-image was reactivated when James Baker was in Israel and the U.S. was being slow in providing $10 billion because of the settlements issue. Raphael Eitan told Baker that "in the previous century you went west and wherever you drove a stake into the ground you said this land was yours. Baker said, That's right. When you talk like this," said Eitan, "they understand."[25]

Like the Americans, the Zionists wished to drive out the indigenous people; the Jacksonian policy of transfer, humane and generous in Jackson's eyes, is relevant here: Greater Israel is today's version of Manifest Destiny.

Other analogies were suggested. Both peoples had fought against a British protector/tyrant; both had created a new society, a new type of human being in a corrupt world. The Zionists were updated Mayflower colonists and the resistance against Britain a modern Tea Party. American terminology was used to show the parallels, and Israel now runs a Friday radio series on Israel's Founders (all of them Ashkenazim). Modern Israel is shown as a mirror of the

U.S.—not a Sephardi or Mizrahi society but one of freedom-loving, individualistic, successful, competent, fun-loving, bronzed and scantily-dressed people. Israel is governed by the Ashkenazim and it is this face which is shown, the cultural and ideological prejudices that are shared with the U.S. that are stressed. Shlomo Swirsky speaks of Israel's "obsessive western orientation"[26] and says Israel presents a western mask. The rhetoric dovetails with the U.S.'s, and the U.S. turns a blind eye to Israel's non-implementation of the stated policy goals, such as democracy, human rights, free enterprise, etc.

Ariel Sharon stated that Israel's forefathers had not gone there to build a democratic state but a Jewish one, yet Israel is consistently portrayed as a democracy. 1992 presidential candidates Tom Harkin, Bob Kerry, Paul Tsongas and Ross Perot all spoke of Israel as a democracy and Bill Clinton charged then President Bush with bullying "the region's sole democracy." Israel's human rights record is poor but is presented as excusable or better than that of others; when Israeli activists informed Congressmen about torture of Palestinians most refused to reply, though one Congressman, requesting anonymity, admitted that the U.S. had "double standards. Israel is not the only one." When the State Department finally started reporting Israel's violations, the Near East Report produced a table, which I give here, showing how good Israel's record on democracy and other desiderata was compared with Arab states'.

	ISRAEL	JORDAN	KUWAIT	SAUDI ARABIA	SYRIA	IRAQ
Democracy	Yes	No	No	No	No	No
Free Press	Yes	No	No	No	No	No
Public Demonstrations	Yes	No	No	No	No	No
Religious Freedom	Yes	No	No	No	No	No
Political Parties	Yes	No	No	No	No	No
Sexual Equality	Yes	No	No	No	No	No

Source: *Near East Report* (February 25, 1991), p. 30.

The NER made the distinction that while Palestinians had suffered at the hands of "Ottoman, British and Jordanian rulers" their present suffering was only a result of "the consequences of their violent intifada against Israel."[27] As to criticism of Israel in the UN, the U.S. has constantly vetoed such criticism and worked to have the Zionism-is-Racism resolution rescinded. Allard Lowenstein was U.S. representative to the UN Human Rights Commission in 1977 but he saw the UN, in its stance on Israel, as a "kind of radicalised Lewis Carroll contraption filled with leftist mad hatters who might next announce that slavery is freedom or that Jews are Nazis, or who for that matter might direct the Mississippi River to flow uphill"[28] and worked to get Z-R repealed.

Israel is able to kidnap, bomb Tunisia, take hostages, hold onto conquered territory and pursue a nuclear programme partly because she has adopted an American mask and an American history. She can violate the U.S.'s stated policy goals and get money, a military partnership and help in disposing of enemies such as Iraq. Criticism of Israel is dangerous. Former Vice President Dan Quayle—with a Defender of Israel Award—attended an AIPAC dinner on 7 April 1992 and addressed diners as fellow Zionists. But he and President Bush were voted out of office as being too pro-Arab, locked into a policy of "appeasement—not devoid of subservience" to the Arab states![29]

Both Israel and the U.S. project a certain construct of history and a certain package of stated policy goals. Neither applies these goals consistently. But when another country is to be punished, its violating of even one of these goals will serve as sufficient excuse. It is indeed hard for any country to implement all these goals, so all are potentially at risk. Also, the very implementing of such goals may harm the country, undermining its traditional culture and economic and social system. Whether the U.S. sees its foreign policy in terms of practical politics and pragmatism (ideas of democracy, flexibility, humanitarian tradition, innovation and trial and error methods versus the Third World's "revolutionary slogans and ideological incantations"[30] or as games theory (where players use rules, signals and ambiguities to get pay-offs), it is vital that other countries internalise U.S.-style values and system. Great attention has been paid to getting the rest of the world to accept the U.S. vision of politics and priorities.

USAID, for example, states that its promotion of U.S. interests is combined with "an American tradition of international concern and generosity." It links its support for the free market and free enterprise with a stated care for democracy, for the environment, and for the peaceful settling of transnational problems and declares that USAID's mission is to "translate into action the conviction of our nation that continued American economic and moral leadership is vital to a peaceful and prosperous world." In this world, countries achieve full potential "through the development of open and democratic societies and the dynamics of free markets and individual initiative."[31] But in his book, *The Ambiguities of Power*, Mark Curtis argues that since 1945 "rather than occasionally deviating from the promotion of peace, democracy, human rights and economic development in the Third World, British (and U.S.) foreign policy has been systematically opposed to them, whether the Conservatives or Labour (or Republicans or Democrats) have been in power."[32] He goes on to describe how direct military intervention, destabilization campaigns, supply of arms to overthrow governments and skillful propagandist reporting in the Western press have been used to this end, and how the academic and supposedly independent media circles ignore the real effects caused by policies designed to satisfy Western business requirements, promoting instead the official ideological agenda. The West does not respect its own stated priorities, though calling on other countries to so do.

But accepting these priorities, believing in the rhetoric, has rarely guaranteed safety. Simón Bolívar found that adopting the federal form of government and "exaggerated precepts of the rights of man" weakened and fragmented the South American republics.[33] The Cherokee nation found that Americanization brought them no favoured treatment: settled farming, schools, Christianity, a written language and a constitution afforded them no protection when Georgia wanted their land.

At the present time the U.S. says it prefers nations "committed to the pursuit of democratic institutions, the expansion of free markets, the peaceful settlement of conflict and the promotion of collective security" and outlaws "backlash states" (Iran, Iraq, Libya, Cuba and North Korea) which do not accept these desiderata.[34] The Palestinians are trying not to be backlash states but to implement these policy goals. This is unlikely to bring them much credit since they are facing what is probably the most pro-Israel administration ever. It could have the effect of shattering Palestinian society.

Edward Said points to this danger, expressing amazement about what he terms a collective Arab amnesia about the U.S.'s history and record on its policy goals and its assault on Arab history and Arab regimes.[35] But the PLO hope that implementing the U.S.'s goals will give them U.S. protection.

As regards free enterprise, the PLO has accepted liberal economic policies and set up a team to this effect. The World Bank has drawn up a report where it is clear that the Palestinian economy will be integrated into the Israeli one, to the Palestinians' detriment. As regards democracy, President Arafat told the European Parliament that the PLO "intend to foster the tradition of democracy practised among our people by building a system based on pluralism, elections, freedom to form political parties, the separation of powers"[36] and a commission has been set up. Criticism is possible inside the PLO, an umbrella organisation: Farouk Quaddoumi publicly came out against the Washington talks and retained his position. But the western media attack Arafat for authoritarianism and the PLO for "unbridled and unaccountable authority."[37] *Reuters* reported how "Palestinian reformists pressing for democratic change within the PLO failed to curb Chairman Yasser Arafat's power."[38] U.S. Council for the National Interest research director Laura Drake said the Palestinians should undergo democracy-education programmes "to instil within the society an instinct to insist on a democratic process."[39]

Women's rights are promoted to undercut the PLO. Although much was done by the PLO to promote the women's cause, Task Force on Women concluded that PLO members were male chauvinists (abus) and that women wanted independence from "male-dominated political factions." Palestinian women were learning, it said, to concentrate not on the liberation struggle but on practical politics—domestic abuse, sexual harassment and personal status issues. "Travel plans are replacing dreams of nationhood." Women's urgent priority was "to defeat Fatah, to make the interim period a failure, and to build a democratic society." International agencies intend to give Palestinians gender-training, seen by the U.S. feminists as a positive development. The greatest danger is not Israel but Hamas and the "patriarchal" PLO.[40] Women's issues are exploited to emphasise the idea of western superiority and push women to reject their own society as backward and oppressive; Arab culture is targeted as peculiarly intolerant. In Leila Ahmed's words: "The presumption is…that Islamic cultures and religion are fundamentally inimical to women in a way that Western cultures and religions are not."[41]

As for human rights, the Unified National Leadership of the Uprising had set up a legal decision-taking process where mediation and reconciliation featured prominently. The U.S. promoted Hanan Ashrawi as head of a human rights commission; when the PLO accepted her and set up its Supreme Palestinian Commission for Human Rights—an "independent body made up of prominent judicial and other Palestinian personalities"[42]—it was told not to interfere. The commission had to be divorced from the PLO. Laura Drake (mentioned above but also on the advisory board of Solidarity International for Human Rights!) said the commission had to be kept wholly independent of the PLO to guarantee "respect for human rights and democracy—they have to keep it absolutely independent."[43] Israel's human rights abuses are less important than possible future PLO ones.

Calls for accountability, women's rights, free speech and commitment to a liberal economic system undermine the PLO, which still has no power or state structures in Palestine. And simultaneously settlements are extended, Palestinians are killed, imprisonments continue and the boundaries of Jerusalem are changed to ensure that Palestinians become a minority there. Dr. Khalil Tubakji, the Palestinian delegate responsible for Jerusalem, says: "The Israelis are in such a hurry to make Jerusalem an entirely Jewish city that they are building frenetically"[44] to be ready for the time when Jerusalem's status is determined. And of course there was the Hebron massacre.

I end with some words of Palestinian disillusion. Perceptions of reality may have begun to pierce the rhetoric. "We have stopped fighting, we have dismantled all our military teams, we have recognised Israel, we are giving everything and we have not received anything until now."[45]

NOTES

1. E. Said, *Orientalism* (London: Routledge, 1978).
2. J.W. Henderson, *The United States Information Agency* (Praeger, 1969) ix; viii; 23.
3. Joseph Duffey, cited in *Wireless File* (July 31, 1993).
4. Henderson, *op. cit.*, p. 16.
5. Dugger, *On Reagan, The Man and His Presidency* (McGraw Hill Book, 1983), p. 248.
6. Henderson, *op. cit.*, viii.
7. Cited by P.D.G. Thomas, *Tea Party to Independence: the Third Phase of the American Revolution* (Oxford: Clarendon, 1991), p. 247.

8. Cited by B. Schwartz, *The Great Rights of Mankind: A History of the American Bill of Rights* (Madison House, 1992), p. 27.
9. Cited by A. Henretta and G.H. Nobles, *Evolution and Revolution—American Society 1660-1820* (D.C. Heath & Co., 1987), p. 139.
10. *Forum* (January, 1993), p. 52.
11. Cited by N. Chomsky, *Year 501: The Conquest Continues* (Verso, 1993), p. 143.
12. N. Chomsky, *op. cit.*, p. 142.
13. Cited by H. Zinn, *A People's History of the United States* (London: Longman, 1980), p. 155.
14. Cited by N. Chomsky, *op. cit.*, p. 26.
15. *Ibid.*, p. 72.
16. *Business Week* ,1975; cited by Chomsky, *op. cit.*, p. 107.
17. Cited by D. Horowitz, *From Yalta to Vietnam* (Harmondsworth: Penguin, 1965), p. 70.
18. H. Melville, *White-Jacket, or the World in a Man-of-War* (1850, New York: Library of America, 1983), p. 506.
19. June 1952 Commencement Address at William Woods College, Fulton, Missouri, cited by A. Edwards, *Early Reagan* (Hodder & Stoughton, 1987), Appendix, pp. 539, 540.
20. H. Zinn, *op. cit.*, p. 183.
21. P. Findley, *They Dare to Speak Out: People and Institutions Confront Israel's Lobby* (Westport, Conn.: Amana Books, Laurence Hill & Co., 1985).
22. *Middle East Labor Bulletin*, (Vol. 4, 2, Spring 1993).
23. C.E. Edwards in *The Link* (Vol. 26, 3, July/August, 1993).
24. Advertisements in *Flame*, P.O. Box 590359, San Francisco, Cal.
25. *Jerusalem Post International* (1 August, 1992).
26. Shlomo Swirsky, "Part of the Middle East? Joining a Regional Alliance," in Dine Horowitz, ed., *The Eastern Aspect: Other News from Israel, Essays from Iton Aher*, April 1993, p. 40.
27. *Near East Report*, (September 6, 1993).
28. A. Lowenstein, *Acts of Courage and Belief* (H.B.J. Publishers, 1983), p. 280.
29. *Jerusalem Post International* (21 December, 1991).
30. C. Crabbe, *American Diplomacy and the Pragmatic Tradition* (Baton Rouge and London: Louisiana State University Press, 1989), p. 258.
31. Agency for International Development (USAID) leaflet, 1997.
32. Mark Curtis, *The Ambiguity of Power: British Foreign Policy since 1945* (London and New Jersey: Zed Books Ltd., 1995), p. 3 and *passim*.
33. *National Geographic* (March, 1994).
34. A. Lake, "Confronting Backlash States," *Foreign Affairs* (Vol. 73, 2, March-April, 1994).
35. Speech to Arab American university graduates in *Mideast Monitor* (14 November, 1992). Clinton charged then President Bush with bullying "the region's sole democracy."
36. Cited in "Leading Economic Role for Europe," *Palestine* (January, 1994), p. 11.
37. *Middle East Report* (January-February, 1994).
38. *Reuters*, January 6, 1994.
39. "U.S. Expert Says Democracy is Key to Palestinian Human Rights," *Palestine* (March, 1994), p. 17.
40. "Palestinian Women's Movement in the New Era," *Middle East Report* (January-February, 1994), pp. 22-25.

41. Leila Ahmed, *Women and Gender in Islam* (New Haven: Yale University Press, 1992), pp. 254, 246 and 248. Citing Elizabeth Fox-Genovese, *Feminism without Illusions: A Critique of Individualism* (Chapel Hill: University of North Carolina Press, 1991), p. 31.
42. "Leading Economic Role for Europe," *Palestine* (January, 1994), p. 11.
43. *Wireless File* (January 8, 1994).
44. Cited in "Race for 'Greater Jerusalem'," *Palestine* (March, 1994), p. 13.
45. Abdel Karim Sidr, PLO local spokesperson in Jericho, cited in *The Guardian* (March 29, 1994).

VICTIMS AND STATISTICS: SUFFERING AND POLITICAL UTILITY

This essay is intended to explore the mechanisms by which victims achieve recognition and status and the way in which public opinion is organised by powerful groups to further agendas which may have little to do with the interests of the victims themselves: victims achieve canonical status when such groups, by addressing a cause; legitimize it. To illustrate the connection between the victims' suffering and the political action which accompanies or results from this suffering, three cases have been probed, one from the 18th century (the Boston Massacre), one from the 19th (the Bulgarian Horrors) and one from the 20th (the Holocaust). The second part of the article addresses the relationship between the very real suffering of the European Jews in the Holocaust and the ongoing "script" within which these sufferings are viewed.

As John Updike says, "The past is as illusory as the future."[1] The canon is the authorized illusion. Such versions of the past, and the control of information and debate, are manipulated to create popular perceptions of the past for today's purposes. Certain key events are highlighted, others eliminated. Victories are particularly celebrated (they spur on to further effort, encourage, unite). But sufferings are useful too and the memories of such sufferings are revived (to legitimize resistance, differentiate, keep hatred alive). The potential power of the victim is great, provided various factors are present. The suffering must be distinguished from the wider mass of human suffering; the agent of such recognition must be a strong, purposeful group; this group must be able to publicize that suffering and demonize the aggressor; there must be action to rectify the situation.

Here it is helpful to make use of the concept of the "hyperreal" as presented by Jean Baudrillard.[2] He explains that events have meaning only as they are read as part of "scripts." The event itself is taken over by the script, which precedes, highlights and appropriates the event. The script is more real than the event, which has to fit into the script or become invisible. Thus the canonical reading is the reading which the ruling group presents of any event; others are marginalized. This is what Noam Chomsky terms "the ability of the powerful to set the terms of discussion."[3]

Victims can only be victims if they are present in the ruling group's script as such. Control of the political discourse gives rise to a consensual political mythology of past and present victims and aggressors. The script is presented as reasonable; the media's use of standard references and assumptions to back up the prevailing political discourse will ensure that whatever the changes in the identity of the real-life victims and villains the script is accepted by the public. The public tends to reject scripts which articulate issues in strategic, Realpolitik terms and favours those based on "idealistic" themes. These themes differ with historical periods. In the eighteenth century, Radical themes of attack on monopoly, tyranny and arbitrary power had great resonance; in the nineteenth, themes of national identity, of fighting the "Other," of preserving white civilisation against a savage onslaught were popular; in the twentieth, ideas of breaking free from the chains of capitalism or alternatively of safeguarding freedom and democracy have provided scripts within which real interests can be pursued. The power group monopolizes this "idealism" and marginalizes other scripts as reflecting the wishes of selfish, narrow interest groups only.[4] Alternatively, the exploiting of victims' sufferings is a method by which a group can gain empowerment.

Thus, not all victims are accepted as such. There are those who are in some scripts victims and in others aggressors (I am thinking here of the Kurds, victims on occasion, exploited and encouraged by Kissinger in the U.S.'s covert action against Iraq in the 1970s and now protected in their safe havens while U.S. and British planes fly over Iraq, communist villains when in Turkey they ask for cultural and political recognition; everything depends on the script.) Then there are the unsung victims (the Tasmans, the Amerindians) whose plight was (naturally, since their existence was a direct threat to the ruling power group) perceived far too late for any righting of their wrong.

There is sometimes a choice of victim: in pre-Civil War America both North and South had "victim" scripts: the North focused on the slaves, and made much of the anachronism, elitism, corruption and savagery of southern society; the South posed as the victim of northern exploitation and oppression and made accusations of northern insecurity, capitalist exploitation, socialism and atheism. British Liberal MP R. Cobden (a proponent of modernisation, thus against slavery) saw the issue as fighting slavery; another, more famous, Liberal, W.E. Gladstone (a proponent of free trade and nationalism) saw the south as fighting for its independence. The winners' scripts have since become canon.

Obviously, writers are selective in their choice of victim. Z. Brzezinsky[5] focuses on victims in non-democratic countries. He assesses that under Hitler over 5 million Jews, 2 million Poles, 6 million Russians and Ukrainians, and 2 to 3 million other Europeans and other categories died, giving a total of some 17 million. Under Lenin and Stalin, 6 to 8 million were directly killed and 20 million killed in labour camps and collectivization, plus 1 million POWs. Under Mao, he estimates 29 million killed. He also mentions the Armenians, massacred by Turks, and those who died in the Hindu/Muslim removals when India and Pakistan emerged.

He pays less attention to the victims of America's friends. Noam Chomsky fills this gap,[6] showing how the 3-million-member Indonesian PKI was wiped out, and hundreds of thousands killed in the invasion of East Timor; how in Guatemala the slaughter of the indigenous population approached genocide; how the South African regime killed some 1.5 million people in neighbouring states. He reviews countries which received U.S. help during their activities or whose officers received training in the U.S. Army's School of the Americas (set up 1946, funded by the Pentagon, still functioning after a 1994 vote).

Further back in history lies a massacre which, while claiming millions of victims, has received scant coverage. Whether unintentional and biological, or intentional and armed, the slaughter "occasioned by the Spanish *conquista* in Peru and Chile may have run as high as 95 per cent of the population, perhaps ten million souls, and the total human population loss of the Western hemisphere may have reached one hundred million in the first two centuries after European arrival. If so, that would have been the worst genocide in human history."[7]

In this paper I intend to take three massacres, each of them part of the Western canon, and show how strong power groups tried with varying degrees of success to exploit them for political ends. I shall consider the Boston Massacre of 1770, the Bulgarian Horrors of 1876, and the Nazi Holocaust. In all these cases there was already an agenda present in the minds of powerful groups, and the victims' sufferings were exploited for the agenda.

THE BOSTON MASSACRE

The Boston Massacre was, compared with the figures we have seen, rather a minor event. Five people were killed. Its importance lay in the way it was manipulated to persuade American colonists that it was time to break away from Britain. Lotfi Ben Rejeb's paper "My Country, Right Or Wrong!"[8] shows how a sense of nationalism did not yet exist but would be created in the fight against a weaker enemy, Barbary; nationalist rhetoric did not describe an existing feeling of nationalism but was intended to will it into existence. Most colonists still felt themselves to be English, with all the rights and liberties of Englishmen. The Massacre was masterminded to break the loyalty most Americans felt to king and country.

After the French and Indian Wars, British troops were stationed in the colonies against possible future fighting with Indians or European powers and to protect customs officials from the mob. In 1769 2 of the 4 regiments stationed in Boston were withdrawn, the troops being unpopular for a variety of reasons: they played martial music on Sundays, drank, behaved as soldiers do, visiting "'Mt. Whoredom' and other red light places"[9] and took local jobs. The people of Boston were in a particularly poor economic state at the time because of the non-importation programme, which hit the poor badly while often being evaded by wealthy Whig merchants; in this situation of economic hardship, soldiers who competed with locals for jobs were strongly resented. British General T. Gage reported on the latent hostility: "The people prejudiced against the troops laid every snare to entrap and distress them."[10]

On March 5, 1770 a large armed crowd led by the Sons of Liberty clashed with British soldiers protecting a sentry guarding a customs house. The mob threatened to fire the barracks and burn the sentry box; fighting ensued and the troops shot five Americans, while the mob dispersed to get their guns. The wealthy leaders who had incited the mob arrived *after* the firing had taken place. The soldiers were acquitted of the charge of murder though two were convicted of manslaughter; John Adams, defending them, argued that they had fired in self-defence.

Here we can glimpse the manipulation of lower class crowds by wealthy Whig merchants and smugglers, as described by D. Hoerder and H. Zinn.[11] These wealthy men trod a dangerous line between encouraging the mob and directing it against the British, and protecting their own opulent homes and wealth from the mob. Was the rioting spontaneous or planned? Previous riots, like the Stamp Act riot, had got out of hand, as described by General Gage: "[t]he Boston Mob, raised first by the Instigation of Many of the Principal Inhabitants, Allured by Plunder, rose shortly after of their own Accord."[12] Major Thomas Moncrieff felt that the rioting had been preconcerted, and Governor Hutchinson, in his account of the events, spoke of the "designs of particular persons to bring about a revolution"[13]; John Adams spoke of "an explosion which had been intensively wrought up by designing men who knew what they were aiming at."[14]

The Massacre was not unusually bloody. Earlier fighting against the Indians had been at least as murderous, and in 1763 the Paxton Boys attacked Indians at Conestoga and killed another 14 Indians at Lancaster. The North Carolina Assembly deemed anyone who refused a court summons for 60 days to be an outcast who could be summarily executed. In 1771 some thousands of Regulators were defeated militarily and six were hanged.

The Boston Massacre was thus an incident—Mercy Warren termed it an "accident" that "arose from a trivial circumstance" and Benjamin Franklin one of a series of "little misunderstandings"[15] that should not cause the British-colonist relationship to suffer or the British Empire to decline. But British conspiracy theorists saw unrepresentative men trying to pervert American loyalty and colonial conspiracy theorists talked of the "deep laid and desperate plan of imperial despotism...for the extinction of all civil liberty."[16] John Adams had early believed in conspiracy: "There seems to be a direct and formal design on foot to enslave all America."[17] Each side had its script. On March 12, the *Boston Gazette* appeared in mourning. *Before* the Massacre, it reported, British troops had been parading the streets with drawn cutlasses and bayonets, abusing and wounding numbers of the inhabitants. An engraving produced and distributed by Paul Revere, "The Bloody Massacre perpetrated in King's Street Boston on March 5th, 1770, by a party of the 29th Regt.," shows British soldiers firing eagerly on the people, while Americans lie in pieta-like swoon.[18] A vast funeral procession for the five victims was organized; perhaps 10,000 out of 16,000 Bostonians attended. Ministers preached on texts such as the "Slaughter of the Innocents." The memory was assiduously kept alive—every year anti-British orations attracted 4-5,000 people.[19]

But the results were in fact meagre. A letter from Annapolis printed in the *London Evening Post* for 28 July 1770 reported that "the late riots in Boston are regarded with a very cool eye all over America except in New England."[20] The trade boycott against Britain collapsed as one by one the colonies opened their ports to trade, and by late 1770 the Customs Board was back in Boston. Castle William was transferred from the colonial militia to the British Army. By 1772, Governor Hutchinson was popular again and J. Adams had refused to prepare an oration in memory of the Massacre. Colonial opinion had not been alienated.

THE "BULGARIAN HORRORS"

I now turn to the "Bulgarian Horrors" so enthusiastically publicized in 1876 by William Gladstone. By mid nineteenth century, Turkey's attempts to raise taxes led to tax riots. The Christian Serbs, Bulgars, Rumanians, Montenegrins and Macedonians were constantly on the brink of revolt. Of the Christian groups, the Bulgars had been allowed an Exarch of their own (1870), which stimulated in them a sense of nationalism. Outside powers saw this as either an opportunity for splitting the Empire and extending Russian authority (the Russian Gortchakov, who wanted this, Disraeli, who feared it) or a dangerous precedent for their own Serb populations (the Austro-Hungarian Andrássy). In 1876, Bulgar guerrillas rose against Turkey; the subsequent atrocities by the Bashi Bazouks, with an official British count of 12,000 dead in one administrative district,[21] were widely reported and commented on first in the *Daily News* 23 June 1876 and then in the British press generally. British politicians proceeded to exploit this massacre for national and domestic political ends.

Disraeli believed Russia to have vast territorial ambitions. To protect the route to India, to minimize Russian influence in central Asia, he needed to preserve the Turkish Empire. Correctly seeing that Pan-Slavists would make war on Turkey on "humanitarian" grounds, he was furious that Gladstone's moralistic approach to the massacre legitimated this pretext. When Russia declared war on Turkey (1877), he sent the British fleet to Constantinople (January 1878), causing Russia to grant Turkey an armistice; and when the March 1878 Treaty of San Stefano offered Russia gains in Asia Minor, Indian troops were called to Malta and Britain, acting with Germany and Austro-Hungary, signed treaties at the Congress of

Berlin that took this newly formed "Big Bulgaria" away from Russia. In the cobweb of treaties that followed, each major power looked after its own interests.[22] The Bulgar victims of the Horrors were not present at the Congress.

While Disraeli minimized the massacre to bolster Turkey, his opponents, for reasons of domestic politics, anti-imperial feeling, future economic penetration of Asia Minor, or religious conviction, presented a barrage of anti-Turkish argument. As E. Said has shown, Turkey represented the crazed, irrational, demonic Other, the antithesis to European order, moderation, balance and development. Enormous publicity was given to the massacres when Gladstone brought out *The Bulgarian Horrors and the Question of the East*,[23] whose original 15,000 copies were reprinted again and again and eagerly devoured by the public. The same year, 1876, saw other contributors offer *New Light on the Eastern Question*,[24] *The Slavonian Provinces of Turkey*,[25] *"The First Alarm" Respecting the Bulgarian Outrages*,[26] and *How to Settle the Eastern Question*,[27] as well as an apologia for Turkey, *The Turks: Their Character, Manners, and Institutions, as Bearing on the Eastern Question*.[28] The issue was, thus, widely debated; in this colonial discourse pity for victims, exercised through public campaigns, was exploited for foreign policy aims and to challenge existing power relations at home.[29]

This literature is one of racist vilification of the Turks, "one great anti-human specimen of humanity"[30] who practice "elaborate and refined cruelty—the only refinement of which Turkey boasts!"[31] The crime assumes mythic proportions: "the basest and blackest outrages upon record within the present century, if not within the memory of man,"[32] "fell Satanic orgies…fiendish misuse of the powers established by God,"[33] and further outrages are predicted: "a new and wide outbreak of fanaticism, and a wholesale massacre…at which hell itself might almost blush."[34] Though the government had treated Christians with a certain tolerance, this is minimised: "Much of Christian life was contemptuously left alone."[35]

Alternative scripts are marginalized. Disraeli's arguments that the Bulgars had risen first, or that there was a measure of guilt on both sides, are considered distortions of the truth; the French translation of a report by the commission of Muslim and Christian notables, approved by the Administrative Council of Philippopolis and presented July 22 to the Turkish Government, is condemned as a "disgraceful document."[36] But the American Commission of

Enquiry, reporting three months *after* the massacres, is presented as neutral. Mr. Schuyler, the U.S. Consul at Constantinople, rebutting Turkey's plea that the outrages were few and often committed by Christians, insisted that the government's statement on this point "and on every other" was a "tissue of falsehoods," yet Gladstone quotes this as impartial evidence.[37] The British Government's support of Turkey is attributed to base motives; Disraeli as a Jew (though christened Church of England) must detest Christian liberty; Gladstone insinuates that Disraeli's Jewishness and his links with European pro-Turkish Jewish communities lie behind his selling of Britain's honour.

The victims are presented as tiny, "brave but raw levies of Serbia"[38] holding out against dreadful odds. But only one paragraph in Gladstone's article, and none in the other pamphlets, proposes help for them. Gladstone's call for relief of "want, disease, and every form of suffering in Bulgaria"[39] is both vague and empty, since he makes it clear that there will be no government money for this.

All solutions to the problem involve the break-up of the Empire. Gladstone proposes that the Turkish administration be excluded from all the small entities (Serbia, Bosnia, Herzegovina, Montenegro and Bulgaria).[40] An anonymous pamphlet proposes that Turkey's fall is "inevitable"[41]; the only question is who will get the pieces; "would it not be wiser to divide the whole of the Turkish Empire among the interested Powers, and entirely supersede the effete and corrupt Ottoman government?"[42] As Turkey has wasted the land, another group should be allowed to make it productive. Syria should go to "the Jews, whose right to possess the land is indisputable.... Naturally the land is theirs, and the Powers would be justified in building up this people."[43] Here the anti-Islamic argument dovetails with Christian fundamentalist reasoning: the Jews should occupy Syria "for the aggrandisement of nations till they be restored" to Palestine.[44]

Aytoun proposes that "the Mahometan government be put an end to in Turkey"[45]; while Muslims rule, Christians will be "tyrannised over and oppressed."[46] The Horrors provide the pretext for a Christian take-over after a legitimizing Parliamentary vote "founded upon the grounds and reasons by which we were actuated, viz. the atrocious manner in which the Christians in Turkey have been treated."[47]

Munro-Butler-Johnston's is the only paper to show how the victims are being exploited and the Horrors manipulated to produce a new victim, Turkey: "History, ethnology, geography, and religion are pressed into the service. The virtues and vices of the victim, his proud indifference, and his culpable carelessness, are alike traded on." The Bulgars' suffering is a cloak for rapaciousness; the cycle of violence will continue, for the Turks "will prefer death to surrender of independent sovereignty."[48]

THE NAZI HOLOCAUST

The rise of Nazi Germany produced millions of victims; European Jews were particularly targeted; millions of Jews were killed, and their story is well known.

I wish to address the use made of these victims. As was stated at the beginning of this paper, we are illustrating a process by which powerful groups make use of victims for their own ends. First, the Nazis tried to make money out of them. Secret negotiations (Jan./Feb. 1938) between G. Rublee, director of the Intergovernmental Committee on Political Refugees, R. Pell, others and an official from the German Ministry of Economic Affairs resulted in a "statement of agreement": there would be a "phased ransoming of German Jewry over a period of three to five years by 'outside' Jews, and the finding of a resettlement haven."[49] But the West dropped the plan.

Another ransom offer was made in 1944. On April 25 Eichmann told Joel Brand to arrange a deal: Germany would trade 100 Jews for a truck; a million Jews for 10,000 trucks and coffee, tea etc. The trucks would not be used against the West but against the USSR. But Churchill wrote to Eden July 11 warning: "There should...be no negotiation of any kind on this subject."[50] The reason given? The Nazis were committing "probably the greatest and most horrible crime ever committed in the whole history of the world."[51] On July 20 the BBC carried the official announcement that the "Jews for trucks" deal was off. When Hitler proposed in July to release the Hungarian Jews to Sweden, Switzerland and the U.S.—but not Palestine—the U.S. took a similar line. Cordell Hull signed for the War Refugee Board that it could not "enter into or authorize ransom transactions of the nature indicated by the German authorities."[52] On November 21 the State Department sent a telegram under Stettinius's signature that "no (repeat, no) funds from any source should be used to carry out such a proposal" but that the negotiations must continue[53]; on January 7, 1945 the WRB telegram said that though 20 million Swiss francs had been transferred by the Joint Distribution Committee none of this could be spent without government approval; the money was being shown "solely" to keep the talks alive, thus "gaining more precious time."[54] As the end of the war approached, several SS heads tried to exchange Jews for trucks and cash. The failure of the attempts is usually presented as the Nazis' fault —"Berlin's zeal to win the last battle against the Jews."[55] But it is obvious that the West had no intention of ransoming the Jews; their excuse was that the offer was a ploy to divide the Allies, or that the main duty was to win the war. Was Zionist reasoning also behind the refusal?

Much has been written on how little the Great Powers did to stop the slaughter of the Jews (or others). But very little has been said about the Zionists' role. British and U.S. politicians and public were unwilling to trade the Jews for war material, unwilling to bomb the death camps or the railways that led there, or to let Jews into their own countries. They did not open their doors, nor did the Zionists ask them to open their doors. The door that was to be opened was that to Palestine. While leaders like Ben Gurion called for millions of Jews to be transferred to Palestine, politicians linked wartime Jewish suffering in Europe to a post-war reward in Palestine.

Winston Churchill was a self-confessed Zionist ("I am strongly wedded to the Zionist policy, of which I was one of the authors"),[56] accused by non-Zionists of committing the "Conservative Party hook line and sinker to the Zionist cause."[57] His diaries and war correspondence[58] say little about the Jews' suffering and where they are mentioned they are linked to *post-war* hopes. He vowed that in the victory deals the Jews' sufferings "will not be forgotten"[59] and related "evil crimes" to post-war hopes. According to Weizmann, (11 March 1942) Churchill promised him that after the war "I would like to see Ibn Saud made lord of the Middle East (the boss of the bosses (provided he settles with you. It will be up to you to get the best possible conditions."[60] Saud "will have to agree with Weizmann with regard to Palestine."[61] He later recommended adding the Negeb to Palestine as a "refuge to the survivors of the Jewish community who have been massacred in so many parts of Europe."[62]

Labour's Hugh Dalton, whose stance was described as "Zionism plus plus," made few references in his diaries[63] to Jewish suffering but gave support for the Zionist agenda, assuring the Jewish Agency liaison agent that the Party supported "unlimited Jewish immigration and rights of Jewish land acquisition in Palestine." His personal preference was "to extend the boundaries of Palestine either into Egypt or Transjordan. There is also something to be said for throwing open Libya or Eritrea to Jewish settlement, as satellites or colonies to Palestine."[64]

In the 1944 and 1948 U.S. elections, presidential candidates linked Jewish suffering to Zionist solutions. Governor T.E. Dewey said that "in order to give refuge to millions of distressed Jews driven from their homes by tyranny, I favor the opening of Palestine to their unlimited immigration and land ownership."[65] Harry Truman (on the national committee of the Campaign for a Jewish Army) called for 100,000 Jews to be let into Palestine; Dewey for hundreds of thousands.

Membership of Zionist groups rose, as did the funds collected. "5,700,000—Did They Die In Vain?" was the slogan for the Dec. 1945 United Jewish Appeal to raise over $100 million for Jewish refugees and settlement in Palestine.[66] In 1943, when B'nai B'rith president H. Monsky sent out invitations to an American Jewish Conference to prepare for the Victory Peace Conference, neither increased immigration into the U.S., nor provision of temporary shelter, was discussed, but only the "post-war status of Jews and the upbuilding of a Jewish Palestine."[67]

Between 1933-9, neither Britain nor the U.S. relaxed its immigration policy. In the U.S., additional restrictions were introduced; Breckinridge Long describes how the State Department used obstacles to "postpone and postpone the granting of visas"; "The list of Rabbis has been closed and the list of labor leaders has been closed...."[68] Offers from Hitler to release Jews were rejected. At the July 1938-February 1939 Evian Conference on Refugees, when the "Federal Representation of German Jews" proposed that German Jews be taken by various countries, most participants, attending after the clear stipulation that none would be required to alter their immigration policies, excused themselves.[69] The Nazis were trying to make the Reich *judenrein* "within the context of emigration and forced extrusion...had there been a will among receiving nations to take in the penniless refugees from the Reich, more might have been saved."[70]

On 27 March 1943 Eden and Hull refused to save 60,000 Bulgarian Jews;[71] later, fear was expressed that the Nazis might "change over from the policy of extermination to one of extrusion, and aim as they did before the war at embarrassing other countries by flooding them with alien immigrants."[72]

When in 1945 President Truman called for 100,000 Jews to enter Palestine, only 4,705 entered the U.S.; not until 1948, when Israel was established and bringing in large numbers of Jews, did the U.S. change its policy and let in between 1948-50 40,000 Jewish DPs.

After the war, in the refugee camps, the Zionists' "message was frankly political: they told the survivors that there was no hope anywhere else, that people had to struggle to open the gates of Palestine to Jewish refugees"[73] and said "the Jewish survivors expressed their strong wish to reach Palestine, and to rebuild their lives in a Jewish state."[74] But H.N. Smith (Lab.), who had visited a camp near Graz, 1947, believed most of its 3,000 Jews wanted to go to the U.S.; "But the Zionists had arranged otherwise."[75] Paul Mason accused the Zionists of setting Jews against other refugees and exploiting bad treatment to pressurize Jews to opt for Palestine. British General F. Morgan, head of the UN Relief and Rehabilitation Administration in Germany, said the same, earning himself vilification and suspension for racial bias. (In fact, his charge was based on intelligence from the U.S.'s 3rd Army; Haganah *was* organising immigration in the camps.[76])

The Holocaust was used to establish the absolute priority of a state for the Jewish survivors and marginalize any claims the Palestinians might put forth. For Yitzhak Shamir, "every individual and every nation" would be judged by its attitude to the Holocaust as reflected in its treatment of Israel: atonement meant support for Israel.[77] C. Clifford used it as his argument, accusing the State Department, unwilling to create an Israeli state, of being "widely regarded as anti-Semitic."[78] Pro-Zionist U.S. Senators warned UN member states that U.S. money and goodwill depended on their behaviour in the UN vote to create Israel. Since then, the Holocaust has repeatedly been exploited to Israel's benefit. She has received large sums from Germany as reparations.[79] *Le Monde* of 13 May 1995 stated that 40% of the total 350 billion francs paid up to 1994 for Holocaust victims had gone to Israel, plus economic and military aid from Germany. The Holocaust is so frequently used to justify pro-Israel action that I give just a few examples here. Rep. Allard Lowenstein wrote that linking F16s for Israel to an arms package for Saudi Arabia reminded "Jews everywhere of Jews who are no longer anywhere" because they had trusted the West.[80] In June 1991 Bush was praised for helping Ethiopian Jews "return" to Israel: "you learned the lesson of the Holocaust."[81] In November, Bush, now an "Arabist," was warned that making Israel surrender land would lead to "a revival of Hitler's genocide programme."[82] In 1992, 73 Senators sponsored unconditional loan guarantees to Israel because "No Jew wants to be remembered for failing to do what was necessary" (leaving the Russian Jews to a second Holocaust).[83]

Now we return to the theme of our own conference. It may no longer be vitally important whether or not the Boston Massacre is taught in the heroic mode; the Bulgarian massacres may be relevant today; but the Holocaust is still of the first political importance, used to validate political action. As Alfred Lilienthal has said, the Zionists' main strength lay in their ability to exploit international public opinion.[84] Control of Holocaust information is thus vital; this means ensuring that the subject is taught widely, in the U.S. especially, and "correctly," and that alternative interpretations are marginalized and their proponents vilified.

Great attention has been paid in the U.S. to providing Holocaust education. In 1972, Friedlander said that the New York Times believed "the annihilation of European Jewry should be a mandatory subject in our public schools"; he opined that schools would rush to "implement the popular mandate"; he complained that in the universities the Holocaust was "offered as a subject only under pressure and without serious intent,"[85] but by 1992, AIPAC's Political Leadership Development Program was liaising with over 200 campuses to rectify this.[86] In 1989 Eliach reports that "almost every city, county, state has its own curricula" on the Holocaust, but wanted more: "In none of the American Indian museums, or the books written about American Indians, did I find any reference to the Holocaust."[87] The Institute for Holocaust Studies was set up in 1979 to "establish Holocaust centers of study in every university and college across the world," and set up Holocaust courses in the U.S. "in all high schools" for "several hours weekly."[88] By 1989 "Holocaust studies are accelerating on campuses throughout the

United States at an unprecedented pace. At present, over 200 colleges and universities are offering courses which deal with the Holocaust."89 In 1980, the Holocaust Memorial Council was set up to sponsor conferences, and "a magnificent teaching Memorial Museum,"90 "the Holocaust Memorial Museum...the most visited museum in the national capital" was opened by 1995.91 Even in primary schools the question is *when*, not *if*, "children should be taught about the greatest evil of modern times—the Holocaust."92

Stress is laid on the *defensive* nature of Holocaust education; it is argued that the U.S. is awash with anti-Semitic and anti-Israel publications which must be countered by, for example, the Institute for Historical Studies. "Among the dangers facing the Jewish people today is the concerted effort of so-called historical "revisionists" to deny the reality of the Holocaust," says the ADL, which then "developed a comprehensive package to counteract the dramatic increase in instructional materials about Israel and the Arab-Israeli conflict which lack historical depth, perspective and balance." The ADL offers 220 books, videos, pamphlets etc. for training in classroom and society. The campus kit contains works on anti-Semitism, Holocaust denial and anti-Israel propaganda, and the Journal of Holocaust Studies is used "extensively as a teaching aid on the elementary and high school levels." The ADL says it has trained "more than 110,000 elementary and secondary school teachers, impacting more than 10 million public, private and parochial school students...[and] reached students at more than 400 college campuses."93

"Correct" teaching[94] means, firstly, that the figure of 6 million Jewish victims is given as canon, and indeed it is always given by the press. The ADL repeats it,[95] calling the "current campaign to deny that Hitler's regime murdered six million Jews" anti-Semitic propaganda. But there *is* room for debate. The recognised authority here is Raul Hilberg, who gives the figure as 5,100,000. Others have suggested 7 million[96] or 3.6 to 6 million[97] or a lower figure.[98] The figure for Auschwitz deaths has fallen from 4 million to 1.1 million ("The larger figures have been dismissed for years, except that it hasn't reached the public yet") or 300,000.[99] Probably one third of Jews world-wide died. Despite the difficulties inherent in assessing deaths, and the existence of various estimates, querying the 6 million figure is presented as anti-Semitic or is ridiculed: "Would they feel better if it were only five million Jews killed or four million?"[100]

The Holocaust is presented as unique, "irreducibly distinct from any other historical event or phenomenon,"[101] an event to which there are no analogies, "sacred history." Alternative versions are "sacrilege"; correct representation a "holy task."[102] Other victims are generally ignored; the Holocaust is the "planned mass murder of the European Jews."[103] In my (fairly wide) reading of Holocaust literature, I found Gypsies mentioned twice, other national groups rarely, homosexuals never.[104] Attempts to universalize the Holocaust (e.g., P. Weiss's *The Investigation*) are indignantly attacked.[105]

Holocaust literature ignores Zionism; the Great Powers' responsibility is stressed, and metaphysical ideas of universal responsibility evoked, but I have found no sense (even Friedlander) that the Zionists had any part in what was happening.

There is an insistence on the endemic nature of anti-Semitism. and the need for an Israeli state to defend Jews. The Zionist argument runs that if the Jews had had a state, the Holocaust would not have happened; or, illogically, that they "were persecuted mercilessly as a nation; they had to be reborn as a nation."[106] Attacks on Israel or resolutions such as the UN Zionism-is-Racism resolution are insults to Holocaust victims. The Holocaust is used to validate Israel's "unique claims upon Jews and non-Jews alike."[107]

Alternative versions, other sufferings, are marginalized. Let us take the Gypsies. From known figures it seems that between 1933-45 1.5 million were killed out of a total world population of 2 million. Subject, like the Jews, to a census, while Jews were sent to separate schools, the Gypsies were removed from all schooling. Intermarriage with Germans was prohibited, as was sex. "Jews, Negroes, Gypsies and bastards" were from 1934 seen as a danger to the purity of the German race; and stricter criteria were applied to identify Gypsies than Jews. From 1933 Gypsies were sent to sterilization camps. From 1939 they were interned in camps and gassed. But no powerful group tried to rescue them or award reparations to the Romani nation; pre-war anti-Gypsy laws and public hostility prevented their sufferings being recognised. The "press gave them scant coverage" and "most of the officials of the Jewish communities considered that these confiscations had only affected Jewish property."[108] When the above-mentioned Holocaust Memorial Council was set up not one Gypsy was among its 65 members; yet it was its President, Elie Wiesel (who blocked every request for a Gypsy presence) who said in 1986, "Silence encourages the tormentor."[109] When in 1985 the Jewish Central Council organised a commemorative ceremony for the liberation of the Bergen-Belsen camp, it refused to let any Gypsy speak. But the absence of reference to the Gypsies in practically all Holocaust literature causes no indignation.[110]

Still less has been written about homosexuals. "It is impossible to give any accurate figure for the total number of people killed by the Nazis solely for their homosexuality,"[111] but at least hundreds of thousands were killed. In Germany, in May 1933, Dr. Hirschfeld's Institute for Sexology was burned, and 20,000 books, mostly from the Institute, destroyed; gay rights groups were outlawed; the mere intent to commit a homosexual act became a crime. In 1942 the death penalty was introduced for homosexuality; any gay in the Army was instantly shot. Earlier than Jews and Gypsies (from 1933) homosexuals were sent to labour and concentration camps, in "level 3" conditions: "We were indeed the lowest caste in the concentration camps, even persecuted and sent to our death by our fellow-prisoners."[112] Only gays worked in the clay-pits of the Klinker brick-works, the "factories of human destruction."[113] In 1942, in Buchenwald, homosexuals were used for medical experiments; in 1944, experiments with synthetic hormones were carried out there; gays were also castrated. Lacking the support of any powerful group, there were no attempts at ransom, and their suffering has since been ignored, unmentioned except in a few specialised journals; "the situation is worse than simple forgetfulness.... Gay people, though a very distinct category in the concentration camps, were even omitted from memorials erected to the victims of Nazism."[114] No reparations were paid. Most gays, whose national laws still made homosexuality a crime, were afraid to tell their story. In France, for instance, the anti-homosexual Law No. 744 of 6 August 1942 was not repealed until 1981, whereas anti-Semitic laws were repealed by De Gaulle after the Liberation. The first public debate in France took place in 1981; after this, gays dared to speak out about their wartime experiences. Neither the Nazis' "Jewish victims nor their victims of the left, in both cases so articulate, have stretched out a hand to us and made known to the world that we homosexuals, too, shared their fate."[115] In the 1,245 pages of the recently reprinted *The Rise and Fall of the Third Reich* there is not one reference to gay suffering—and this book is praised for its objectivity.[116] Had the author omitted Jewish suffering he would have been labelled a revisionist historian, yet his excision of gay suffering passes unchallenged. When Chief Rabbi Immanuel Jakobovits can simultaneously complain about the "cloak of respectability" hiding "fake historians who deny the Holocaust" and denounce sodomy as an abomination, calling for homosexuality to be made a criminal offence,[117] this neglect should surprise no-one.

As alternative versions are marginalized, "revisionists" are reviled, equated with anti-Semitism. For the expensively produced *Anti-Semitism World Report*, in 1992 "Jewish security throughout the world is perhaps affected most seriously of all by Islamic fundamentalist groups"[118] (cf. the Nation of Islam and its publications)[119]—which may be the case—though the Report admits to "insufficient knowledge" here; or the enemy is the "rabidly anti-Semitic pseudo-historians and academic charlatans" and "'institutes' that are generously financed by well-known extreme Rightist and neo-Nazi organizations."[120] Now though I have read a liberal supply of "correct" Holocaust literature, I have found it extremely *difficult* to locate anti-Semitic works. At the Cambridge University Library I located one "major" threat, the IHR's "pseudo-scholarly" *Journal of Historical Review*. It is a small, cheaply printed journal, since 1992 not kept by the Library. Another "major" danger is David Irving; the Library stocks works in which he speaks of the concentration camps and persecution of the Jews, but I could not locate the book— *Hitler's War*—for which he is reviled. Can the *JHR* and Irving represent a major threat when it is so difficult to find their work? Irving is simultaneously "among the most dangerous" because he has "the trappings of a respectable historian," is a good researcher and is the "darling of neo-Nazi activists,"[121] and an "amateur historian" with "no academic qualifications as a historian."[122] Presented as a fascist "nutter," his conclusions are thereby invalidated. Fined by a German court for denunciations of stories of mass extermination (in France and Germany Holocaust denial is illegal),[123] he is banned from several countries; his October 1993 invitation to speak at four Irish universities was cancelled for fear of reprisals.[124] "Reputable" publishers do not handle his work and, since he is increasingly denied access to archives, his research is being restricted. Another stifled critic is C.D. Edwards, whose programmes on CBC, KPFA and KALW-FM were discontinued, the sale of his cassettes stopped, and his 1969 talk at the College Association for Public Events and Services cancelled because of pressure.[125]

From the time of Morgan and Bevin,[126] anti-Zionism has been presented as anti-Semitism.[127] The argument that Illinois's mandating of Holocaust education in its public schools is possibly unconstitutional is treated as anti-Semitism.[128] Advertisements in student papers for a fresh look at the Holocaust are deemed anti-Semitic; it is argued that only those whose motives are inspired by hatred would wish to debate the subject. Removal of work from display, wrecking of offices, silencing and vilification are methods whereby the canon is protected. A neutral researcher must associate with groups which are sufficiently committed (pro-German, Islamist, marginal) to risk being branded anti-Semitic. One finds strange bedfellows.[129] Uncommitted persons who fear contamination from contact with such groups will remain uninformed. My argument is not that these groups are *right*, but that their literature is *extremely difficult to acquire*, while there is an abundance of "canonical" literature on the subject.

In spring 1996, the "abbé Pierre" affair erupted in France when the abbé Pierre, up until then widely admired for his work among the poor, and on the comité d'honneur of the Ligue contre le racisme et l'antisémitisme, was attacked for his support of a book by Roger Garaudy—*Les Mythes fondateurs de la politique israélienne*.[130] Among other things, the book questioned the Holocaust figure, addressed the relationship between the Holocaust and the state of Israel, and spoke of the power exercised by Zionism over the American and French media. Though it was admitted that Garaudy's book was not negationist but revisionist, it was banned by big French bookshops such as the Fnac and other books by Garaudy were removed from sale. Dominique Jamet wrote that it was "à peu près introuvable et plusieurs organes de presse, la semaine dernière, se sont étonnés qu'il soit disponible dans certaines librairies et ont demandé qu'il soit retiré de la vente, exigence qui semble avoir été suivie d'effet."[131] Garaudy was prosecuted for infringing the 1990 Loi Gayssot by the MRAP (Mouvement contre le racisme et pour l'amitié entre les peuples). When the abbé Pierre suggested a debate on the accuracy of Holocaust research and proposed that from being victims the Jews had themselves become killers (of Arabs), he was subjected to furious media criticism on the grounds that he was relativizing the Holocaust; his stance was presented as a new form of the old Roman Catholic conspirationalist anti-Semitism.[132] The Union des étudiants juifs de France asked President Chirac to strip him of his Légion d'honneur. Cardinal Lustigor's definition of the issue as "une attaque contre la politique israélienne, et, dans la foulée, contre le sionisme et les juifs en général"[133] confused three rather different elements.

Two years later, in 1998, a change had taken place. New views of Israel's history and origins, especially the expulsion of Palestinians and destruction of Palestinian villages, proposed by radical Israeli historians such as Benny Morris, Avi Shlaim and Ilan Pappé, were presented to French readers in D. Vidal's and J. Algazy's work[134] and Zeev Sternhell's book, *The Founding Myths of Israeli Nationalism, Socialism and the Making of the Jewish State*[135] was translated into French. Zionism was shown to be related to other (exclusivist) East European nationalisms, and the words of Ben Gurion were quoted to reveal a decision to clear the lands of Palestinians for Jewish settlement: "le seul souci qui doit imprimer et dominer notre action est la conquête de notre terre et son redressement par une énorme immigration. Tout le reste est rhétorique."[136] Much of what was written was similar to that found in Garaudy's book. But the Vidal book was praised by former Israeli ambassador to France Yehuda Lancry as being objective, balancing new ideas against the official Zionist narrative, recognising that Israelis had to open up to the Palestinian myths and narrative; it would, he opined, present a setting for Israeli-Arab peace and reconciliation.[137] An advertisement for the book appeared in *Le Monde Diplomatique*, May 1998. At last, it said, the French public could read a new, radical, non-official presentation of post-Zionist debate: "En France, elle est presque inconnue: aucun des livres consacrés par ces chercheurs iconoclastes à la guerre de 1948-1949 n'a été traduit."[138]

Why was it necessary for French readers to await the publication of works by Israeli writers? These writers were indeed opposed to the canonical view of Israeli history. But it seemed that a critical review of Zionist mythology could be undertaken by Israelis alone; the charge of "revisionism" was reserved for other critical versions.

NOTES

1. J. Updike, *Memories of the Ford Administration, A Novel* (London: Hamish Hamilton, 1992), p. 313.
2. J. Baudrillard, *The Evil Demon of Images* (Sydney: Power Institute Publications, 1987) and other works. Hyperreality is where models and scripts become more

real than the real. Helpful also is Gearóid Ó Tuathail's "Foreign Policy and the Hyperreal: The Reagan Administration and the scripting of 'South Africa'," in T.J. Barnes and J.S. Duncan, eds., *Writing Worlds: Discourse, Text and Metaphor in the Representation of Landscape*, (London and New York: Routledge, 1992), which shows how tiny Nicaragua can be presented as a threat to the U.S., or terrorism as a major danger. Consider also how Iraq was presented as about to make a nuclear attack on the U.S.: "We are dealing here with our own survival. As soon as Iraq gets the bomb and the missile, millions of American lives are in peril." (W. Safire, "Assume the Iraqi Bomb Is Just Around the Corner," in the *International Herald Tribune*, 8 November 1990).

3. J. Pilger, "Newspeak Economics," in *New Statesman and Society*, 3 March 1995.

4. In the U.S., the Arabs or the oil lobby have often been presented as dictating foreign policy. For example, in debates on Palestine in the UN, it was proposed that the public- and Congress-supported pro-Zionist line was being sabotaged in the Arab interest by unrepresentative U.S. foreign policy chiefs, who used the UN "not out of any dedication to its principles and prestige but for the sake of narrow national goals" (K.R. Bain, *The March To Zion*, [College Station and London: Texas A & M University Press, 1979], p. xvi).

5. Z. Brzezinsky, *Out of Control: Global Turmoil on the Eve of the 21st Century* (New York: Charles Scribner's Sons, 1993), pp. 10-17.

6. N. Chomsky, *Year 501: The Conquest Continues* (London and New York: Verso, 1993).

7. D. Stannard, *American Holocaust: Columbus and the Conquest of the New World*, quoted in R Hughes, *Culture of Complaint: the Fraying of America* (Harrild: Oxford University Press, 1993), p. 101.

8. L. Ben Rejeb, *"My Country, Right Or Wrong!" American Nationalism: The Making of a Tradition, c. 1785-1815*, lecture given 12 April 1995, *passim*.

9. R.A. East, *John Adams* (Boston: G. K. Hall & Co., 1979), p. 42. The quartering of troops, accepted in Britain, where a quartered Army meant possible husbands and certain custom, was resented by the colonists, who, while hoping for custom and patronage, did not want to offer any contribution to their own defence. Benjamin Franklin mentioned a commonly-held view that quartering was customary but illegal—"as they think, contrary to Law." (Benjamin Franklin, *Essays, Articles, Bagatelles, and Letters, Poor Richard's Almanack, Autobiography* [New York: Literary Classics of the United States, Inc., 1987], p. 853). But when in September 1768 Sam Adams tried to get the Massachusetts Convention to resist the arrival of the Army, the vote went against him, and 28 September two regiments entered Boston harbour.

10. P.D.G. Thomas, *The Townshend Duties Crisis, The Second Phase of the American Revolution 1767-1773* (Oxford: Clarendon Press, 1987), p. 180.

11. D. Hoerder, "Boston Leaders and Boston Crowds, 1765-1776," in *The American Revolution: Explorations in the History of American Radicalism*, ed. A.F. Young (DeKalb: Northern Illinois University Press, 1976), describes how the Whigs destroyed anti-boycott petitions while themselves evading the blockades, and mobilised crowds while themselves avoiding arrest; "none of the Whig leaders was ever brought to justice. The latter in fact even got a man indicted who had condemned the riots." (p. 257) While Whigs contained lower-class dissent, they "thundered against the dangers of standing armies and submission to unlimited authority". (p. 160) H. Zinn, *A People's History of the United States* (London and New York: Longman, 1980), pp. 57-70 shows how wealthy colonists tried to divert resentment away from themselves and against Britain.

12. Zinn, p. 65

13. T. Hutchinson, *The History of The Province of Massachusetts Bay, From 1749 To 1774, Comprising a Detailed Narrative of the Origin and Early Stages of the*

American Revolution (London: John Murray, 1828), p. 290. Hutchinson says that the Boston town committee report, with the "variance of their account of the facts from the statement of the whole evidence, as it afterwards appeared in the trials, is a strong instance of the small dependence which can be placed upon *ex parte* witnesses, examined by men engaged in political contests" (p. 277). Reports sent by the meeting to politicians in Britain attributed the stationing of troops in Boston to "the intrigues of wicked men, with design to enslave it." Hutchinson points out that only two out of hundreds of witnesses saw guns fired from the custom-house and that the two were of unreliable character, one being a disreputable French boy and the other an idiot.

14. Thomas, p. 181.

15. Mercy Warren, *American Revolution*, I, pp. 92-93, quoted in L.H. Cohen, *The Revolutionary Histories: Contemporary Narratives of the American Revolution* (Ithaca, New York: Cornell University Press, 1980), p. 72. R.W. Clark, *A Biography, Benjamin Franklin* (New York: Random House, 1983), p. 256. Franklin assured Lord Chatham that he had not heard in the colonies "the least expression of a wish for a separation, or hint that such a thing would be advantageous to America."

16. L.H. Gipson, *The Coming of the Revolution, 1763-1775* (New York: Harper & Brothers, 1954), p. 203, quoting from the 15 May 1770 Boston town meeting.

17. 1765, quoted in J.H. Hutson, *John Adams and the Diplomacy of the American Revolution* (Lexington: University Press of Kentucky, 1980), pp. 34-35. Hutson comments that scholars have observed paranoia and intense suspiciousness among pro-Revolutionary patriots. Cohen describes how American conspiracy theorists tried to prove that Britain intended to enslave them, whereas Loyalists such as J. Galloway stated that "the people in the Colonies were more free, unencumbered and happy than any others on earth" (J. Galloway, *Historical and Political Reflections on the Rise and Progress of the American Rebellion* [London, 1780], pp. 3-5, quoted in Cohen, p. 153); certain Americans were conspirators—a "dangerous combination of men" (Cohen p. 155) and Jonathan Boucher saw the colonists generally as "the dupes of a few desperate democrats in both countries, who thus misled them (as it is the hard fate of the people always to be misled) merely that they might be made their stepping-stones into power." (J. Boucher, *A View of the Causes and Consequences of the American Revolution* [1797], p. xv; quoted in Cohen, p. 259) P.C. Hoffer, *Revolution and Regeneration: Life Cycle and the Historical Vision of the Generation of 1776* (Athens: University of Georgia Press, 1983), p. 10, comments on the "apparent chasm between the fearful warnings of the revolutionaries and the actual indignities entailed in the parliamentary regulatory acts of 1764-74"; P. Shaw, *American Patriots and the Rituals of Revolution* (Cambridge, Massachusetts: Harvard University Press, 1981), p. 24, shows how it was an article of faith for patriots that a malevolent design "against the freedom and purity of America" lay behind British actions.

18. L.H. Gipson, *op. cit.*, p. 202, note 22. The engraving appears as plate 20.

19. P.D.G. Thomas, *Tea Party to Independence, The Third Phase of the American Revolution 1773-1776* (Oxford: Clarendon Press, 1991), p. 223. Thomas describes the cautious policy of General Gage, who placed no restrictions on patriots' access to Boston and permitted anti-British sermons, such as that given by Dr. Joseph Warren to an audience including S. Adams, J. Hancock, and British Army officers.

20. Thomas, *The Townshend Duties Crisis*, p. 198. And C. Hibbert, in *Redcoats and Rebels: The American Revolution Through British Eyes* (New York: Avon Books, 1991), p. 16, quotes the *New York Gazette*: "Property will soon be very precarious. It's high time a stop was put to mobbing."

21. R.C.K. Ensor, *England 1870-1914* (Oxford: Clarendon Press, 1936), p. 44. The Bashi-Bazouks committed the massacres in May and June; none were punished and some were rewarded. In July, Serbia declared war on Turkey. But, as so often with massacres, the numbers were disputed; the American Consul in Constantinople, Schuyler, estimated 15,000 at the "lowest."

22. Russia kept Rumania and Bulgaria (northern); Austria-Hungary occupied Bosnia-Herzegovina: (a) it was kept out of Russia's hands, (b) it would not be a Serb state, threatening the integrity of Austria-Hungary. Britain occupied and administered Cyprus. Turkey kept the Macedonian vilayets and a province in central Bulgaria under a Christian governor and had to work with Britain—with whom a defensive alliance was made—to protect her Christian populations.
23. W.E. Gladstone, *The Bulgarian Horrors and the Question of the East* (London: John Murray, 1876). It was printed at 6d the copy. It castigates the Government, especially for its idea of "equality of guilt," praises the courage of an article in the *Daily News* of 23 June, predicts further outrages, and demands the total withdrawal of Turkey from Bulgaria, Bosnia and Herzegovina. It was followed by open-air speeches and political agitation.
24. *New Light on the Eastern Question, or, The Future Centre of Commerce* (London: E. Marlborough & Co., 1876). Also at 6d a copy, it called for a compromise between Russia and the Great Powers to divide up Turkey proper and Turkey's Asiatic dependencies.
25. *The Slavonian Provinces of Turkey; an Historical, Ethnological, and Political Guide to Questions at Issue in These Lands*, (London: Edward Stanford, 1876). 1/- the copy, it warns against Russian attempts to get quasi-independent states in European Turkey, which would fall under Russian tutelage.
26. *"The First Alarm" respecting the Bulgarian Outrages* (London: William Ridgway, 1876), 3d the copy.
27. J. Aytoun, *How to Settle the Eastern Question* (London: Hardwicke & Bogue, 1876). At 6d the copy, it suggests that Russia and Austria-Hungary conquer Turkey; this will be cheaper than letting Britain fight.
28. H.A. Munro-Butler-Johnstone, M.P., *The Turks: Their Characters, Manners, and Institutions, as Bearing on the Eastern Question* (Oxford and London: J. Parker & Co., 1876). At 1/- the copy, it is a rather orientalist pamphlet but pleads for the integrity of Turkey. In *The Eastern Question* (1875), reprinted from the *Pall Mall Gazette*, he argues that it is of vital importance to Britain to maintain the Turkish Empire.
29. *Cultural Studies*, ed. L. Grossberg, C. Nelson, P. Treichler (London and New York: Routledge, 1992), p. 245. The slavery issue was also used by those who intended to gain empowerment by taking up the cause of the slaves, by texts, lecture tours, etc.; as William Knibb said in 1832, "(t)here is nothing more delightful than to stand forward as the advocate of the innocent and persecuted."
30. Gladstone, *op. cit.*, p.9; an "advancing curse."
31. *Idem*, p. 18.
32. *Idem.*, p. 8.
33. *Idem.*, pp. 27 and 31.
34. *Idem.*, p. 23.
35. *Idem.*, p. 9.
36. *Idem.*, p. 19. The Turkish Government naturally clove to this document, which said that the Bulgars had risen against paternalist Turkish rule, committing atrocities such as roasting and impaling victims, and intending "to massacre the Mussulman population," and that the reports of the Massacres were lies, unverified reports, etc. Though this report could well have been produced under pressure, its reference to Bulgar atrocities was certainly credible.
37. *Idem.*, p. 24.
38. *Idem.*, p. 23.
39. *Idem.*, p. 32.
40. Here Gladstone offers, alongside the moral line of reason, a pragmatic justification: if Britain does not do this, the Russians will, and if the Christians of these mini-states see Russia as their saviour "the command of Russia over the future of

Eastern Europe is assured" and thus the whole purpose of Disraeli's maneuvering will be defeated.
41. *New Light on the Eastern Question*, p. 25.
42. *Idem.*, p. 26.
43. *Idem.*, p. 29.
44. *Idem*. The entirety of Turkey should be divided up; the religious justification (speeding up Christ's Second Coming by bringing the Jews back to Jerusalem) and the economic (the fertile land is not being developed; modern commerce and penetration require a different framework, which the commercially-minded Jews will provide) marry.
45. Aytoun, *op. cit.*, p. 3.
46. *Idem.*, p. 4.
47. *Idem.*, p. 7. He suggests that Russia and Austria be allowed to overrun and conquer Turkey and rule it, thus substituting a Christian for a Muslim government. For Britain it will be cheap because Russia and Austria will do the fighting!
48. Munro-Butler-Johnstone, p. 35. After giving a glowing, though rather orientalist, description of Turkish civilisation, he points out that though Europe denounces Turkey for making religious wars, it is doing precisely the same. Here it is interesting to note that Ensor's work, a textbook, describes the 1912 war against Turkey in similar terms: "These victories pleased all lovers of freedom, because they liberated a large area of mainly Christian population from the hideous misgovernment of the Turk" (p. 464).
49. H.L. Feingold, "The Government Response" in H. Friedlander and S. Milton, eds., *The Holocaust: Ideology, Bureaucracy, and Genocide: The San Jose Papers* (New York: Kraus International Publications, 1980), pp. 246-7. The San Jose Conferences were held in 1977 and 1978, sponsored by the National Conference of Christians and Jews.
50. R. Hilberg, *The Destruction of the European Jews* (New York: Holmes and Meier, 1985), p. 1139. While half a million Jews were being killed in Auschwitz, Eichmann had promised that a first hundred thousand Jews would be released, and if the trucks and cash came as promised, the others would follow. Other reports on the Brand deal are found in Rabinowicz, Bauer, etc. (see below).
51. O.K. Rabinowicz, *Winston Churchill on Jewish Problems* (New York: Thomas Yoseloff, 1960), p. 132.
52. Y. Bauer, *American Jewry and the Holocaust: The American Jewish Joint Distribution Committee, 1939-1945*, (Detroit: Wayne State University Press, 1981), p. 414.
53. *Idem.*, p. 424. Bauer remarks that dragging out the negotiations probably saved up to 17,000 Hungarian Jews to survive. The Hungarian offer is also described by B. Vago in "The Horthy Offer: A Missed Opportunity for Rescuing Jews in 1944" in R.L. Braham, ed., *Contemporary Views on the Holocaust*, Holocaust Studies Series (Boston: Kluwer-Nijhoff Publishing, 1983), pp. 23-40; Vago only says that "America, in spite of intended goodwill, was too slow to react effectively and not resolute enough to act without the British" (p. 40).
54. Bauer, p. 428.
55. Feingold, p. 246.
56. In *Roosevelt and Churchill: Their Secret Wartime Correspondence*, ed. F.L. Loewenheim, H.D. Langley and M. Jonas, (London: Barrie & Jenkins, Ltd., 1975), p. 54. Also, "No one has done more to build up a Jewish National Home in Palestine than the Conservative Party," hoping that it would "develop into a Jewish State," 29 January 1949, *Hansard*, p. 952. It must be remembered that Churchill had expressed anxiety about Roosevelt's Atlantic Charter, where "in the Middle East the Arabs might claim by majority they could expel the Jews from Palestine, or at any time forbid all further immigration" (Loewenheim, p. 54).
57. H.N. Smith, 26 January 1949, *Hansard*, p. 1006.

58. Loewenheim; also Rabinowicz; also B. Gardner, *Churchill In His Time* (London: Methuen & Co. Ltd., 1968); also M. Gilbert, *The Churchill War Papers* (London: Heineman, 1993); also D.J.C. Irving, *Churchill's War: The Struggle for Power* (Bullsbrook: Veritas Publishing Company Pty. Ltd., 1987); also J.P. Lash, *Roosevelt and Churchill 1939-1941: The Partnership That Saved The West* (London: André Deutsch, 1977).

59. Rabinowicz, p. 107, gives Churchill's November 1941 message to the Jewish Chronicle, and his October 29, 1942 message to the London Albert Hall meeting.

60. Rabinowicz, p. 139. Rabinowicz wonders why Churchill did not then announce an immediate partition plan and let in large numbers of Jews.

61. Irving, *Churchill's War*, p. 566; the Cabinet papers for May 19 1941 say there should be self-government, with "provisions for expansion in the desert regions to the southward."

62. 26 January 1949, *Hansard*, p. 956.

63. *The Second World War Diary of Hugh Dalton, 1940-1945*, ed. B. Pimlott (London: J. Cape, 1986); also, T.D. Burridge, *British Labour and Hitler's War* (London: André Deutsch, 1976).

64. Pimlott, p. 799; 26 October 1944, Dalton reassured the agent that the Labour Party Declaration on Palestine would be backed by the U.S. Democrats and Republicans; the April 1944 NEC International Committee resolution, which offered the Arabs compensation and resettlement elsewhere, worried some Labour Members, who feared the Zionists would expect the next (probably Labour) Government would do everything they wished (p. 739) and asked "why the Jews shouldn't all go to the British Empire and the U.S.A. Why need they go to Palestine?" Dalton's suggestion that the Jews go to Libya and Eritrea was made on 7 October 1943 (p. 672).

65. J.A. Rubin, *Partners in State Building: American Jewry and Israel*, (New York: M.P. Press, Inc., 1969), p. 114.

66. Rubin, p. 191. Donations from Jewish groups rose markedly from 1945 ($35 million) to 1948 ($135,500,000) (the idea of an independent Jewish state had obvious appeal).

67. Hilberg, p. 1120. The invitation: "American Jewry, which will be required in large measure to assume the responsibility of representing the interests of our people at the Victory Peace Conference, must be ready to voice the judgment of American Jews along with that of other Jewish communities of the free countries with respect to the post-war status of Jews and the upbuilding of a Jewish Palestine." The war was far from ended but there is nothing about the destruction of European Jewry, giving a warning to Hitler, etc. When the Conference met in August, non-Zionists found the ground cut from under their feet as Zionist resolutions were added to humanitarian resolutions which the non-Zionists proposed. Y. Bauer (*Out of the Ashes: The Impact of American Jews on Post-Holocaust European Jewry* [Oxford: Pergamon Press, 1989]) shows how the Joint Distribution Committee's policy changed from supporting resettlement of Jews in the Dominican Republic, Bolivia or the Philippines, or help in readapting Jews to their pre-war homes, to supporting regular immigration or "immigration to Palestine Israel" (p. xxii).

68. Feingold, p. 253. Feingold describes the link between anti-Semitism and isolationism, the duality of the U.S.'s policy, the differing priorities, but makes no mention of a Zionist angle. The U.S.'s policy was based on the 1924 National Origins Act, whereby 2% of the number of each European national group living in the U.S. in 1890 could enter the U.S. each year. Hundreds of bills were introduced each year to cut immigration. During the war years, only 10% of the possible Jewish quota entered the U.S. The Wagner-Rogers Bill of 1939 proposing that 20,000 minors enter the U.S. was rejected by Congress (*Jerusalem Post International*, November 4, 1989).

69. J. Felstiner ("The Popular Response" in *The Holocaust: Ideology, Bureaucracy, and Genocide*, p. 263) describes the unwillingness to allow Jews to immigrate into the U.S. and shows that only Holland and Denmark agreed to accept more Jewish

refugees. *insight*, Special Edition: "The Holocaust: Facts and Fiction," 1994, p. 3, shows how the U.S. promised to take in 27,370 approved by the American Jewish Agency; Britain said it had no suitable territory; Australia did not want to import a racial problem; Costa Rica and Panama announced they would not accept traders, money lenders or intellectuals, etc.

70. Feingold, pp. 246-47.

71. Loewenheim, p. 73. The excuse was that if the Bulgarian Jews were saved then world Jewry might ask for the German and Polish Jews to be saved and "Hitler might take us up on such an offer and there simply are not enough ships and means of transportation in the world to handle them." In fact, over the Nazi period, Britain let in permanently 70,000 Jews and the U.S. 180,000 (Sir Herbert Morrison, 31 July 1946, *Proposals for the Future of Palestine, July 1946-February 1947*, Cmd. 7044, 1947, H.M. Stationery Office, p. 4).

72. Felstiner, p. 264. *The Guardian Weekly*, April 16, 1995, tells how a secret offer made by Britain to send 5,000 Jewish children to Palestine was dropped when the Germans insisted they went to Britain instead.

73. Y. Bauer, *Out of the Ashes*, p. 44.

74. Y. Gutman and C. Schatzker, *The Holocaust and Its Significance* (Jerusalem: Zalman Shazar Center, The Historical Society of Israel, 1983), p. 219.

75. *Hansard*, 26 January 1949, p. 1007. Smith ("I am not an anti-Semite") is rare in that he mentions Zionist aims and tactics and "Zionist finance located in the United States" (p. 1008).

76. Mason supervised the refugee question for the Foreign Office. His charges are confirmed by Earl G. Harrison's plea in his 31 August 1945 Report (he was the American representative at the IGCR) that the U.S. Army was treating "the Jews as the Nazis treated them except that we do not exterminate them," (*Near East Review*, Nov. 5, 1990) that the other prisoners were asking for segregated camps, and that 100,000 Jews should be allowed to go to Palestine (Bauer, *Out of the Ashes*, p. 48). Morgan's claim stirred up a storm of abuse: M.A. Dohse, *American Periodicals and the Palestine Triangle 1936-1947* (Michigan: Ann Arbor, 1969), p. 192, shows how he was called anti-Semitic by Weizmann and a Nazi by Rabbi Stephen Wise, how *The New York Times* printed Eddie Cantor's article about him "I Thought Hitler Was Dead," how on radio W. Winchell called for the British Government to repudiate him, and how he was suspended by H.W. Lehman, governor of New York state, and F. La Guardia, UNRRA directors general. (Also described in E. Sanbar, *Palestine 1948, l'Expulsion* [Washington D.C.: Institut des études palestiniennes, 1984], p. 116.)

77. *Jerusalem Post International*, 19 May 1990.

78. R.H. Curtiss, "Truman Adviser Recalls May 14, 1948 U.S. Decision to Recognize Israel" in *The Washington Report on Middle East Affairs*, May/June 1991, p. 17.

79. Hilberg (pp. 1178-1183) describes how between 1953 and 1966 Germany paid 3,000 million DM to Israel. In 1953, Albert Norden (East Germany) said Israel had no right to reparations since it was a military base of the U.S., not the legal successor of the Jewish victims. There have been more recent complaints: Helmut Kohl's 1994 candidate for the presidency Steffen Heitmann said, "The genocide of the Jews should not result in Germany having to play a special role until the end of history" and sought to relativize Auschwitz. The resulting outcry forced him to stand down (*Guardian Weekly*, 12 February 1995 and *The Independent*, 26 January 1995).

80. A. Lowenstein, *Acts of Courage and Belief* (H.B.J. Publishers, 1983), p. 279.

81. *Near East Report*, ed. M. G. Bard, 3 June 1991.

82. *Jerusalem Post International*, 2 November 1991.

83. *Near East Report*, 10 February 1992. In the *NER*, 2 March 1992, Sen. Bob Kasten warned Americans against believing their administration; as Roosevelt had misled Americans over the Nazis' killings, so Bush was misleading them over Israel's

need for loan guarantees: a pogrom was likely in Russia, and the Holocaust must not be repeated.

84. Alfred Lilienthal at the 6th International Islamic Seminar for Youth, quoted in Abu Fares' unpublished paper "The General Strategy of Jewish Imperialism," p. 11.

85. H. Friedlander, "Postscript: Toward a Methodology of Teaching About the Holocaust" in *The Holocaust: Ideology, Bureaucracy, and Genocide*, pp. 323, 325.

86. *Near East Report*, 27 January 1992.

87. Y. Eliach, "On the Crossroads of Holocaust Studies Forty Years Later" in *The Holocaust Forty Years After*, Symposium Studies vol. 22, ed. M. Littell, R. Libowitz and E.B. Rosen, (Lewiston: The Edwin Mellen Press, 1989), p. 126.

88. J.P. Eisner, "The Genocide Bomb," in R.L. Braham, ed., *Perspectives on the Holocaust*, Holocaust Studies Series (Boston: Kluwer-Nijhoff Publishing, 1983), p. 162.

89. J. Bendremer, "Surveying Holocaust Attitudes: Forty Years After," in *The Holocaust Forty Years After*, p. 81.

90. F.H. Littell, "Holocaust Education After '40 Years in the Wilderness'," in *The Holocaust Forty Years After*, p. 2.

91. L.L. Langer, *Admitting the Holocaust: Collected Essays* (Oxford: Oxford University Press, 1995), p. 11.

92. E.K. Whitehouse, "Deliver Us from Evil—Teaching Values to Elementary School Children," in the *International School Journal* (vol. xv, no. 1, Nov. 1995), p. 23.

93. All the quotations are from the *Anti-Defamation League Material Resource Catalog*, September 1994, pp. 23, 33, 38, 40.

94. Friedlander, in *The Holocaust: Ideology, Bureaucracy, and Genocide*, p.334, shows how L.S. Dawidowicz believes that only Jews can teach the Holocaust; Dawidowicz's book, *The War Against the Jews, 1933-1945* (Harmondsworth: Penguin, 1977), proposes that the Second War was *about* the Jews.

95. *Anti-Defamation League*, p. 23,26,30, etc.

96. Dohse, p. 194. Max Lerner said the central lesson of the fascist adventure was the "seven million" Jews killed.

97. W.F. Renn, "What German Children Learn About the Holocaust in German Textbooks" in *The Holocaust Forty Years After*, p. 108.

98. *insight*, Special Edition, 1994, points out that it is impossible to say how many Jews were murdered, since many would have died in the same way as other civilians. Hilberg points out that at the Eichmann Trial the figure was 5 million; that in 1945 the Institute of Jewish Affairs in New York City gave the figure as 5,600,000; that Jakob Leszczynski of the World Jewish Congress gave the number as 5,978,000; "exactness is impossible" (Hilberg, 1201, 2). In 1945 the Jewish Agency for Palestine gave the figure as 5 million (Rabinowicz p. 163, citing the Memorandum Submitted to the United Nations Conference on International Organization, San Francisco). Israeli Professor Yehuda Bauer highlights the difficulties for assessing deaths (How far is normal life expectancy a factor? How much was due to a generalized fear leading to flight? Or to population shift? How far did Jews suffer *as other groups*?) Prof. Bauer admits that figures he gave in previous books were sometimes wrong (*Out of the Ashes*, p. 36).

99. *insight*, Jan./Feb. 1994, p. 10, quoting Bauer, reported in the 12 November 1989 *New York Times*. The 300,000 figure is "as stated by the Red Cross after the war." *The Independent*, 23 January 1995, shows how Soviet investigators estimated until 1989 that up to 4 million people had died in Auschwitz, whereas newer figures give 1.1 million.

100. *insight*, May/June 1994, quoting Rafe Meir, "Truth Beats Trials in War Against Racism." Or, as the respectable historian E.J. Hobsbawm puts it (*Age of Extremes: The Short Twentieth Century, 1914-1991* [London: Michael Joseph, 1994],

p. 43): "Would the horror of the holocaust be any less if historians concluded that it exterminated not six millions (the rough and almost certainly exaggerated original estimate) but five or even four?"

101. Friedlander, in *The Holocaust: Ideology, Bureaucracy, and Genocide*, p. 327: "There have been attempts to impose serious restrictions on discussions of the Holocaust by those who wish to elevate the subject to the level of sacred history and who denounce opponents for sacrilege."

102. Friedlander, *idem*, referring to a conference in Jerusalem in 1970, where Emil Fackenheim stated that "the rescuing for memory of even a single innocent tear is a *holy task*."

103. Bauer, *American Jewry and the Holocaust*, p. 17.

104. Friedlander is the only writer I have read who makes comparisons with other groups: he mentions the Turks (the Armenians), and the U.S. (the Indians, the Japanese Americans, the African slaves, Vietnam). He echoes the words of A. Morse replying to Fackenheim: for any person, "that war in Vietnam or that instance of racial injustice is his Holocaust of the moment" (p. 333).

105. L.L. Langer, "The Literature of Auschwitz" in *Admitting the Holocaust*, p. 98, criticises Weiss for neglecting to identify the Jews as the primary victims, and foresees future problems with readers who do not know that the 6 million were Jews.

106. Gutman and Schatzker, p. 220.

107. I. Goldstein, *Transition Years: New York–Jerusalem, 1960-1962* (Jerusalem: Rubin Mass, 1962), p. 134. Goldstein believes that "the Jew...the target of a religiously indoctrinated prejudice, will for a long time to come continue to be exposed to anti-Semitism" (pp. 134-135).

108. S. Weisenthal, *Jews and Gypsies*, Appendix IX in *Amaré Bari Bati*, unpublished, p. 5. Weisenthal is unusual in his recognition of Rom suffering. He gives full details of their persecution, as does T.O. Odley, author of *Bari Bati*, who shows how remaining legislation and public hostility stopped many Gypsies leaving the detention camps.

109. Whitehouse, p. 25. Wiesel said this as he was awarded the Nobel Peace Prize in 1986; Weisenthal writes that all the efforts by the International Association of the Roms to have a Gypsy on the Holocaust Memorial Counsel (sic) were fruitless; every letter to Ronald Reagan ended up on Wiesel's desk. Weisenthal suggested replacing one of the over 30 Jewish members with a Gypsy, and it was only after Wiesel left the presidency that a Gypsy representative was allowed. When Wiesel was awarded the Nobel Peace Prize in 1986, Gypsy organizations decided to demonstrate in Oslo against this bestowal of the prize.

110. O.T. Odley, *Amaré Bari Bati*; D. Kenrick and G. Puxon, *The Destiny of Europe's Gypsies* (London: Chatto Heinemann for Sussex University Press, 1972) are rare in addressing the slaughter of the Gypsies. Such books are difficult to find.

111. H. Heger, *The Men With the Pink Triangle* (London: Gay Men's Press, 1980), in David Fernbach's introduction, p. 14. Michel Tournier, quoted in Pierre Seel, *Moi, Pierre Seel, déporté homosexuel* (Paris: Calmann-Lévy, 1994), p. 191, note 55, writes in *Gai Pied*, no. 23, fév. 1981: "...on parle toujours de l'holocauste des juifs, on ne parle jamais de celui des homosexuels.... Il y a eu huit cent mille personnes massacrées pour fait d'homosexualité." Fernbach shows how few reports were made until 1967, when W. Harthauser's article "The Mass Murder of Homosexuals Under the Third Reich" appeared in an anthology. E. Kogon, *The Theory and Practice of Hell: The German Concentration Camps and the System Behind Them* (New York: Octagon Books, 1973), also addressed the subject. M.B. Duberman, M. Vicinus, and G. Chauncey, eds., *Hidden from History: Reclaiming the Gay and Lesbian Past* (Harmondsworth: Penguin Books, 1991), shows how gay history is ignored. But recently studies such as R. Plant's *The Pink Triangle: the Nazi War Against Homosexuals* (New York: Henry Holt, 1986), have provided more data.

112. Heger, p. 101.

113. *Ibid.*, p. 39.
114. *Ibid.*, p. 8. P. Seel describes how homosexuals were not wanted at official ceremonies in France; there were instances of interference with homosexual wreath-laying; at Besançon there was a cry: "Les pédés au four" (p. 166) and in Paris the gay delegation could only lay its wreath in Notre Dame *after* the official wreath-laying.
115. Heger, p. 15. Seel describes the difficulties in having reparations paid in France: only in 1990 did the *Journal officiel* envisage paying reparations—if the necessary dossier was compiled. Two eye-witness reports of Seel's internment in Schirmeck were necessary for his deportee status to be recognised! (pp. 167-168). Only in 1988 did the German Parliament agree to set up a fund for the "last victims"—homosexuals, gypsies and euthanasia victims (p. 197, note 71).
116. P. Tatchell, "No place in history for gay victims of Nazism," in *The Independent*, 2 July 1995, believes that W. Shirer's *The Rise and Fall of the Third Reich*, 1960, should be amended "to present an accurate history of the Nazi terror."
117. *The Independent*, 27 January 1995; and C. Bermant, *Lord Jakobovits* (London: Weidenfeld and Nicolson, 1990), p. 175. In 1988, he became the first rabbi ever to be given a British peerage.
118. Quoted in *Commentary*, October 1994, "The Jihad Against the Jews." In this article Martin Kramer agrees that "the greatest threat today comes not from neo-Nazis but from those fundamentalists of Islam who see in every Jew a political target in their war against Israel" (p. 42). B. Lewis, *Semites and Anti-Semites: An Inquiry into Conflict and Prejudice* (London: Weidenfeld and Nicolson, 1986) argues that the special Arab outrage about Israel derives not from the displacement of Palestinians, nor the central position of Jerusalem, but from the *identity* of the Jews—"Nazi-type anti-Semitism came to dominate Arab discussion of Zionism and Judaism as well as the state of Israel" (p. 240); "...classical anti-Semitism is an essential part of Arab intellectual life at the present time" (p. 256), though it lacks the visceral, personal hostility of European anti-Semitism.
119. For example, *The Secret Relationship Between Blacks and Jews*, 1991. E. Pollack says the Nation of Islam "framed their argument round a free speech issue—should people be allowed to say this on college campuses?" The American Historical Association denounced any suggestion in the book that Jews played a disproportional role in slave labour exploitation. ("Jewish Role in Slave Trade 'Distorted'," *Guardian Weekly*, 26 February 1995.)
120. Eisner, in *Perspectives on the Holocaust*, p. viii. Also Bendremer complains (*The Holocaust Forty Years After*, p. 81) about the Institute for Historical Review with its "pseudo-scholarly" *Journal of Historical Review*.
121. *Anti-Defamation League Catalog*, p. 23.
122. *Journal of Historical Review*, Jan./Feb. 1993, vol. 13, 1, p. 17. (Only Friedlander believes he should be heard and refuted.)
123. *Ibid.* In Germany, denial of the Holocaust carries a penalty of up to 5 years in prison ("'Mark of Cain' lingers in national consciousness," *The Guardian*, 28 Jan. 1995). H.J. Cargas reports in *Holocaust and Genocide Studies* (Oxford: Pergamon Press, 1986), p. 8, that "a British journalist suggested that a law should be passed in all lands to make it a crime to say that the Holocaust never happened. He received an ovation for that remark."
124. *insight*, Jan./Feb. 1994, p. 5. Trinity College, Galway and Cork, and University College Dublin. In G. Stern's "Let Him Speak," *Literary Review*, April 1996, p. 10, Irving is quoted: "In my view the Nazis murdered up to a million Jews (shot them into pits, etc.) and allowed probably another two million to die through criminal negligence (typhus epidemics, lack of sanitation, overcrowding, starvation)." Critics say his views are "appalling".
125. C.D. Edwards. His article in *The Link*, July/August 1993, vol. 26, no. 3, gives a full account.

126. Bevin is accused by Rubin (p. 123) of "anti-Semitic rage" because Bevin had warned that if the Jews tried to get to the head of the refugee queue there was the danger of another anti-Semitic reaction. In *Hansard*, 29 January 1949, Smith states (p. 1004) that "Some hon. Members confuse anti-Semitism with anti-Zionism."
127. This perhaps explains why I have been unable to obtain, from three publishers, T. Segev's, *The Seventh Million: The Israelis and the Holocaust* (New York: Hill and Wang, 1994), which charges Zionists with seeing the Holocaust only as it served their cause, and terming survivors "undesirable human material."
128. F.H. Little, *Jerusalem Post International*, 30 June 1990.
129. I myself would not give this talk in the West. I have been warned off by Palestinians, friends and family. I have no wish to be sacked from my job, like Malcolm Ross (*insight*, July/August 1991, p. 3; September 1991, pp. 6; 7. Fired from his job of 18 months by the New Brunswick Human Rights Board of Inquiry, Ross was later reinstated when it was shown that he had never expressed his anti-Semitic views in class [*insight*, Jan./Feb. 1994, p. 14]. The President of the Canadian Jewish Congress said the ruling would be appealed in Canada's Supreme Court), nor ruined by lawsuits, like Ernst Zundel, tried in Canada and Germany for questioning the 6 million figure, (*insight*, Jan./Feb., March/April 1994. Ernst Zundel was sentenced in 1985 for saying 6 million Jews had not been killed; he was retried in 1988 and tried in November 1991 in Germany), or Fred Leuchter, deported from Britain, jailed in Germany and released to prepare a defence in Massachusetts for his Report on the use of Zyklon B; (*insight*, July/August 1991, p. 9. Fred Leuchter's Report on the death camps was challenged by the Beate Klarsfeld Foundation. In *Truth Prevails: Demolishing Holocaust Denial: The End of "The Leuchter Report,"* ed. S. Shapiro [New York: Beate Klarsfeld Foundation, 1990], Leuchter is reproached for bringing "samples of illegal chippings gathered without permission" [p. 3] and exposed "as neither a chemist nor toxicologist nor an engineer" [p. 9]. The court case lasted from December 1990-June 1991. Leuchter said he wanted an international team to do the same investigation he had done: "I want them to prove me wrong or agree with me" [*insight*, April 1991, p. 8.]) I do not want to see my lecture engagements cancelled like those of Irving, or my office destroyed, as was that of the Institute for Historical Research in 1984 (*The Spotlight*, 11 January 1993, claims that the IHR office was burned down by Israeli agents on 4 July 1984), or of a pro-Palestinian group in Long Island University (*Jerusalem Post International*, 29 February 1992. Bobby Brown, interviewed on campus tactics, "struggles to keep a straight face" as he describes how the office was "destroyed one night.") I dislike having to search the works of neo-Nazis for information and trying in vain to acquire books by such persons as Tom Segev or Marc Ellis, who argues that the Holocaust is a powerful tool for policing the American Jewish community and questions the "almost sacred assumption"—that of the relationship of the Holocaust to the state of Israel (cited p. 223 of the *Journal of Historical Review* [vol. 12, no. 2, Summer 1992] ed. M. Weber, reviewing M. H. Ellis's *Beyond Innocence and Redemption: Confronting the Holocaust and Israeli Power* [New York: Harper and Row, 1990]. Ellis discusses how Holocaust theology is distorted, exploiting the victims.) Because of this difficulty, I decided to address myself to the guardians of the canon, the Jewish groups themselves. In March 1995 I wrote to fifteen U.S. Jewish or Zionist organizations with 2 simple questions: what is now the figure for Jewish Holocaust dead? Which states mandate Holocaust education? Most did not reply. Six envelopes were returned unopened. Hadassah replied but said they could not help me; they recommended writing to the Zionist Archives and Library, or the American Jewish Historical Society, neither of which replied. The National Christian Leadership Conference for Israel did reply. Its letter said that the number of Jews slaughtered was "probably even more than six million," referred me to Bauer, asked the ADL to mail me their catalogue and said Holocaust teaching was mandated in *all* New Jersey schools. Other states (Florida, New York, California) mandated the subject but lacked the necessary infrastructure.

130. R. Garaudy, *Les Mythes fondateurs de la politique israélienne* (Paris: la Vieille Taupe, 1995).
131. D. Jamet, "L'Histoire re relève pas des tribunes," *L'evénement du jeudi* (*EDJ*), 27 June-3 July, 1996.
132. P.-A. Taguieff, "L'héritage de la judéophobie," and C. Askolovitch, P. Cohen and V. Maestracci, "La victoire des révisionnistes," *EDJ, idem.*
133. *Libération*, 21 June 1996.
134. D. Vidal and J. Algazy, *Le Péché Originel d'Israél: L'Expulsion des Palestiniens revisitée par les "nouveaux historiens" israéliens* (Paris: Editions de l'Atelier, 1998).
135. Z. Sternhell, *The Founding Myths of Israeli Nationalism, Socialism and the Making of the Jewish State* (Princeton: Princeton University Press, 1998).
136. Z. Sternhell, quoting Ben Gurion in 1922, in *Le Monde Diplomatique*, May 1998, p. 4.
137. Y. Lancry, *Le Monde Diplomatique*, May 1998, p. 4.
138. *Le Monde Diplomatique*, May 1998, p. 3.

JEWISH IMMIGRATION AND A JEWISH ARMY: BRITISH AND AMERICAN APPROACHES

Britain's and the U.S.'s conflicting attitudes towards Jewish immigration into Palestine and a Jewish Army can be viewed under three major headings: as a function of the overall context of the country's attitude to Zionism; as an example of how practical, day to day constraints and outside stimuli affected policy; and as an illustration of how each country's self perception and assumptions about the world provided a context within which specific policies were defined and applied.

Britain was committed to a Zionist programme and gradually lost her taste for it. Her first commitment and later recoil were dictated by military and strategic calculations. The U.S., initially unwilling to interfere, later pressed for a Zionist policy regardless of foreign political considerations. Britain could change her policies without regard for domestic reaction; the U.S.'s policies were by the 1940s almost entirely directed towards satisfying domestic demands.

Britain was more suspicious of Zionist intentions than the U.S. and tried to balance her Zionist commitment against other foreign considerations. The Balfour Declaration and the stated aims of the Mandate were frequently criticised (by the House of Lords, the military, Foreign Secretary Curzon, officials in Palestine, etc.).

The U.S. under Woodrow Wilson's presidency had given the Declaration secret support and in 1923 recognised Britain's Mandate; few, apart from the King-Crane Commission, expressed disquiet and little attention was paid to other foreign policy calculations.

Britain's policy under the Mandate brought increasing unrest until, by the time of the 1939 London Conference, Colonial Secretary Malcolm MacDonald had to tell the Zionists that Britain was being forced by practical necessity to change her policy. Moshe Sharett, then head of the Jewish Agency's political department, called the Conference a plot, intended to show the Arabs Britain was on their side.

By the 1940s Britain had begun to fear the Arabs might turn to Germany (and, later, the USSR) and endanger Britain's position in the Middle East. There was oil to be considered, and relations with Egypt, and the effect on India's government, which had a large Muslim population to consider.

Indeed, there was every reason to fear. German and Italian radio propaganda made much of Britain's fighting Arabs in Palestine and beamed this to the Arab world. As Miles Lampson, later in the CIA, had warned both Britain and the U.S.,

> unless the Arabs get satisfaction over immigration we must face the fact that, if war comes, we shall have to take on the Arabs as well as the Italians and Germans.[1]

In 1945 a Labour government came to power with a strong pro-Zionist platform which it immediately abandoned. It believed that Britain's responsibilities in the Mideast were overstretched and hoped to evolve a new policy, jointly with the Arab states, of defence and development for the region. It promoted the idea that Britain was now to deal with "peasants not pashas" and it wanted the defence system to be agreed on and implemented by Britain and the Arabs acting as a bloc, not as individual countries. The logical consequence of this policy was the idea that Britain should not imperil her interests in Suez and Abadan and the Mideast generally by failing to attend to the nationalist sentiment that was gaining ground in the region—and to the Palestinians' desires in particular. Foreign Secretary Ernie Bevin saw the Mideast as a region second in importance only to Britain herself and was afraid that loss of Arab goodwill would eliminate British influence there (to the advantage of the USSR). And loss of British influence in the Mideast would weaken the Commonwealth as a whole.

Britain also foresaw the danger that allowing a religious state to be formed in Palestine would augment the risk of the Muslim Brotherhood pressing for one in Egypt.

She also thought that there was no logical certainty as to how a future Jewish state would behave, since Yugoslavia, Czechoslovakia, Poland and the USSR were all helping to run illegal arms and immigrants into Palestine. Bevin thought that the USSR was sending indoctrinated Jews there to turn Palestine into a Communist state, or to balkanise it; either prospect was bad for Britain. Even if the state did not immediately turn to the eastern bloc, it could use the possibility of its doing so to blackmail the west financially and territorially. Indeed, suspicion seemed to be justified when the Arab countries, after the partition vote and quick Soviet recognition of Israel, sacked Communist institutions as well as American ones: in Damascus the Soviet office was attacked and the Communist Party headquarters stormed.

Britain had come so far from her first Zionist commitment that she opposed the 1947 UNSCOP plan: it would antagonise the Arabs, said the 18 September Cabinet report, just when "our whole political and strategic system in the Middle East must be founded on cooperation with those states."[2] Then she let the question go to the UN where she wrongly assumed the vote would go against partition (the eastern bloc she expected to vote as usual against the U.S.) and herself abstained on the vote. She refused to implement the partition resolution. In 1948 the editor of the *Times* quoted Arab League Secretary General Abdul Rahman Azzam as saying he thought Britain had been ready to take a fairly strong anti-Zionist stand (as in the 1939 Command Paper) but had been bullied by the Americans. (But some thought he was a British stooge who would say anything!)

This was Britain's other major consideration: the attitude the U.S. The state of her war-shattered economy left her dependent on U.S. help. Winston Churchill, a committed Zionist, made much of the fact that the Arabs' friendship was worth less than what U.S. hostility would cost Britain. It was clear what the U.S. wanted. New York mayor Fiorello La Guardia pointed out that if Britain wanted U.S. loans, she should keep her promise on the Balfour Declaration.

The U.S. had supported Zionism since before the Balfour Declaration and the Mandate but had done little to promote it. Her interests were more to do with business (primarily oil) than with geographic, military concerns. But when the Zionists turned their full attention on the U.S., after 1939, the Zionist lobby started to exercise enormous pressure on the administration. This pressure was so great that, for example, the U.S. delegation at the UN (said Chief of Near Eastern Affairs Division Gordon Merriam) never knew what to say because they had no idea what the next bombshell from the White House would bring. McNeil said the Zionists were always given enough time to "put the screws" on Truman when a policy they disliked was under consideration (the leaking of the Morrison-Grady plan was followed by such Zionist outrage that the plan was dropped). Truman himself said of the UN vote that he had never before experienced such pressure.

Britain, herself dependent on the U.S., realised to what extent the U.S. president was dependent on the Zionists. "The United States had long been interested in Palestine, but it was not until 1945 that American interests in Palestine and pledges made in America became one of the determining factors.... The whole question of who should be elected to certain offices in the United States turned on this problem," said Bevin,[3] also remarking that Truman's attitude in 1948 seemed to be Jewish expansion whatever the cost.

The British government was less affected by Jewish voting power; there were fewer Jews in Britain.

The U.S. administration was pro-Zionist for certain foreign policy calculations, too. It wanted to remain strong in Russian eyes and criticised what Clark Clifford called "shilly-shallying appeasement of the Arabs" during the war. It also wanted to keep the old imperialist powers out of the Mideast—the setting up of the Arab League was seen as a British trick, and Britain was seen as a rival for Arab oil. It signed a pact with Britain in 1944 agreeing on the principle of equality of opportunity, to break Britain's near monopoly in the Near East. It feared any UN involvement which would let the imperialist powers into the Mideast through the back door. After the partition vote it became increasingly fearful of Soviet intentions. But fears of an Arab reaction were rarely expressed, and when the State Department and the Chiefs of Staff pointed out the risks to U.S. oil, educational and commercial interests in the Mideast implicit in the policy the administration was following, and said that the Soviet Union was preparing to extend its social and economic system there, the administration preferred to call the State Department "anti-Semitic" and write off its fears.

In 1944 the military was horrified at the violently pro-Zionist tone of Congress resolutions, fearing this would lost them Arab friends. While Franklin D. Roosevelt was in power and the war was on, this sentiment was respected. But under Truman, both military and State protests were ignored. In vain did the Chiefs of Staff warn Truman that the whole of the Middle East was threatened with violence if immigration into Palestine continued.

What distinguished the U.S.'s commitment to Zionism from that of Britain was that, as well as foreign policy calculations and Zionist pressure, another factor affected its attachment to Zionism: for years the American people had supported the idea of a Jewish state. (It is interesting to note that British politicians never referred to British popular wishes on the Mideast issue but always to former government declarations and papers, whereas the U.S. constantly harped on the theme that it was reflecting the will of the people.)

Presidents Roosevelt and Truman made it clear that their policy reflected popular sentiment. F.D. Roosevelt stated in his 1944 "Dear Bob" letter to Senator R.F. Wagner that "the American people support this aim" (of establishing a Jewish commonwealth)[4] and H. Truman wrote in his letter to King Ibn Saud that the "American people have supported the concept of a Jewish home in Palestine since the first World War."[5] Rabbi Steven S. Wise could say without fear of contradiction that Zionism equalled Americanism. Ernie Bevin noted that most Americans saw Zionists as following in the footsteps of the Founding Fathers. The Anglo-American Report commented that everywhere among the Arabs there was almost complete identification of the United States and Zionism. And Miles Copeland said that American diplomacy in the Arab world after 1947 consisted in trying to "convince the various Foreign Offices that our government was not under the control of the Zionists,"[6] while Amin al-Husseini compared Congress to a Zionist tool: "No one ever thought that 140 million Americans would become tools in Jewish hands," he said in 1944.[7]

The Americans supported Zionist ideas and the Zionists made sure that this remained so. In 1947 Rudolph G. Sonnebom, a Zionist working in Palestine, admitted that "we have at least one person in virtually every community in America."[8]

To show how Zionists could be found in every category of American society a quick glance will suffice. The granges and unions had supported Zionism since the early 20th century (the AFL in its 1917 resolution stated that Zionist claims were legitimate); the leaders were pro-Zionist and the rank and file had a sentimental attachment to the ideal of the Histadrut as a dynamic union movement in an ideal socialistic society. By 1945 the Communist Party of America said it supported the "just" demands of the Jewish people to rebuild their homeland and slammed the "imperialist" British White Paper of 1939. Workers were led to sympathise with Zionist ideas because the very people who had brought about pro-labour legislation in the U.S. (Wagner of the Wagner Act and Fiorello La Guardia of the Norris-La Guardia Act, for example) were fervent Zionists. Progressive figures such as R.M. La Follette and L.D. Brandeis were also well-known for their Zionist feelings, and Brandeis—a Supreme

Court judge—legitimised Jewish immigration into Palestine and Haganah activities by his approval. Another Supreme Court judge, Felix Frankfurter, gave legal cover to Zionist ideas. The courts in general felt the same way.

Access to college education for Jews was far higher in the U.S. than in Britain, so more prominent figures were Jewish and therefore potential Zionists. Colleges and universities (where Hebrew had long been taught) were sympathetic to Jewish concerns; 150 college presidents signed pro-immigration petitions. City and local governments were frequently run by pro-Zionist figures: in New York, where the Jewish vote was high, mayors Herbert Henry Lehman and Fiorello La Guardia promoted Zionism. In 1939, thirty state governors supported the Balfour Declaration and condemned Britain's White Paper. Business federations and Rotary and Kiwanis clubs and both Catholic and Protestant clergy supported Jewish immigration into Palestine. Even in a little town like Meriden, Connecticut, whose total Jewish population was 1,500, 12,000 people sent letters to the administration calling for Jewish immigration into Palestine. Showbiz figures like Billy Rose and Ben Hecht organised pageants and rallies. Even gangsters ran arms to Palestine for the Zionists and gave large financial contributions. Even OSS men like James Jesus Angleton helped smuggle illegal arms and refugees into Palestine.

That is not to say all Americans were strict ideological Zionists. But public opinion polls showed broad backing for Zionism and widespread underlying sympathy for the European Jews and support for their return to Palestine, whereas in Britain there was little popular support for Zionism and the well-known Zionists were politicians or bankers and mainly Jewish (Winston Churchill, Harold Wilson, Sir Herbert Samuel, Sir Mark Sykes, Herbert Bentwich and Lord Rothschild). The British Labour Party had been able to totally ignore its election promises and introduce a non-Zionist policy in Palestine without causing a public outcry. But American presidents had to compete with pro-Zionist pronouncements to get re-elected, as will be seen when comparing stances on immigration.

Now we turn to the practical, day by day, aspect of implementing a policy (or policies) on immigration and a Jewish Army.

Immigration was the tool with which the Zionists intended to settle the land, build up an armed force and ultimately take power. The Palestinians recognised the threat and as early as 1891 a number of Jerusalem notables asked the Grand Vizier in Istanbul to prohibit further Jewish immigration. Britain, trying to implement the incompatible promises in the Balfour Declaration and Mandate, was unsure of the justice of allowing increasing Jewish immigration, was afraid of losing the sympathy of the Arab world and India and was caught in the dilemma of how to balance Jewish and Palestinian desires. Her policy shifted according to circumstance. She also drew a clear distinction between the long-term problem of Jewish immigration and the specific post-war problem of Jewish refugees.

Early on, British politicians realised that Zionist assurances that immigration would not harm the Arabs were not to be depended on. As Chaim Weizmann talked in 1917 of freedom for all Jews to emigrate to Palestine, Foreign Secretary Lord Curzon and Sir William Joynson-Hicks warned that Weizmann should be checked and that there was a danger that thousands and thousands of Jews would enter Palestine. Joynson-Hicks said that the Palestinians should be able to have an immigration policy of their own. The 1921 British Commission of Enquiry said the Jaffa riots had been caused by Arab fear of immigration; the British knew the Arabs were afraid that immigration would lead to a Jewish state.

The Conservative Party supported immigration. Winston Churchill admitted later that "many of us have always had in mind that this might some day develop into a Jewish State."[9] Clement Davies said that, because the Jews were so few in Palestine, "the object was to encourage them to go there, and when, ultimately, they were in a position to do so, a State might then be formed."[10]

While immigration raised the Jewish population from 57,000 (1917) to 384,000 (1936), it was clear the much-talked of 'benefits' were going to be fairly one-sided. Despite Churchill's insistence in his 1922 memorandum that "immigrants should not be a burden upon the people of Palestine as a whole, and that they should not deprive any section of the present population of their employment,"[11] land once bought by the Jewish National Fund could never revert to Arab ownership, Jewish labour was used instead of Arab and the Histadrut did not accept Arab members. The British Commissioner for Palestine, writing to the Colonial Secretary, informed him of the Palestinians' fear that the Jews "in the not too distant future [they] will gain economic and political control of the country."[12]

Discontent, riots in 1929-30 and the 1936-9 rebellion forced Britain to reconsider her immigration policy. The Passfield White Paper (1930) banned further immigration, though the next year saw a retreat from this position as a result of the furious Zionist reaction. The 1936-37 Peel Commission limited immigration, though stating that this was to be temporary only. The 1939 White Paper set a ceiling: 10,000 would enter over the following five years per year, with perhaps an extra 25,000, and after that none, unless the Palestinians agreed. Thus Britain responded to events when designing policy; before this, the only limit on immigration had been the country's "absorptive capacity."

That phrase had been Churchill's. The 1922 Command Paper had stated that immigration should not exceed the "economic capacity of the country at that time to absorb new arrivals" (estimated by Britain).[13] There was a vague hope that if immigration was thus limited the country could be "improved" and the Palestinians themselves would see the benefits and accept such improvement. The idea persisted until the 1930s and explains the 1933 Transfer Agreement between the Zionists and Germany: rich German Jews would be allowed out of Nazi Germany with their assets; they would go to Palestine (and there buy German produce) and this would expand the Palestinian economy and thus encourage Britain to increase the quotas of Jews allowed in, on the grounds that the country's absorptive capacity had increased. (The Agreement failed.)

The 1937 Commons Report had suggested that 8,000 could be let in between August 1937 and May 1938 "provided that the economic absorptive capacity of the country is not exceeded."[14] But this approach to the issue was dropped. The Statement of Policy (Cmd. 6019, 1939) said that though this policy had been stated in 1931 in J. Ramsay MacDonald's letter to Weizmann "where it was laid down as a matter of policy that economic absorptive capacity was the sole criterion," it had been decided in 1939 that this was no longer so. Reference had now to be made to whether or not immigration harmed the Palestine economy or political position and decisions made accordingly. Since Arab fears of Jewish immigration led to insecurity of life and property, expense for Britain and bitterness between the Arab and Jewish communities, decisions on immigration could not be made on grounds of absorptive capacity alone. The Command Paper continued (page 9) that "If in these circumstances immigration is continued up to the economic capacity of the country, regardless of all other considerations, a fatal enmity between the two peoples will be perpetuated, and the situation in Palestine will become a permanent source of friction amongst all peoples in the Near and Middle East."

The White Paper proposed a vast increase of immigration temporarily and then a halt. If the Jewish population could be kept to one-third of the Palestinian, this would reassure Palestinians and persuade the Zionists to lower their sights to a more realistic level (accepting that their hopes of a State would not materialise) and get them to start working with the Palestinians. (Not surprisingly, the White Paper was seen as a betrayal by the Zionists. They turned their attention to the U.S.)

In fact, because of the outbreak of World War II, Jewish ration continued after the 70,000 figure was passed.

Debate as to whether Jewish immigration should be promoted took on a new, emotional, content after the war broke out. A link could now be made between the long-term (Zionist) immigration project and the specific issue of saving Jewish lives. Unlike the U.S., which confused the two issues in one passionate whole, Britain saw two separate problems. She also needed to keep her Arab friends from going over to Germany or Italy. The Defence Secretary for Air had said in 1938 that the Mideast would be untenable with a hostile Arab population. To keep Arab support, Britain's stand on immigration had to be made clear. Civil servant Freya Stark explained the British position to the Egyptians ("We have there promised, I explained over and over again, not indeed an end to immigration across the Palestine borders, but an end to its imposition by force and against the majority's consent") and Iraqis and Syrians ("If we did break our promise, I would resign tomorrow; and so would a lot of other people.")[15]

But even as government and ministers tried to keep Arab support in the war, the U.S. was pressuring Britain to "save" vast numbers of Jewish refugees, and British MPs from both parties called for free immigration into Palestine. The murder of large numbers of European Jews gave this call urgency.

After the war ended, the Labour Party was caught between two imperatives: pleasing the U.S. (which held the purse-strings) and letting in up to 100,000 Jews immediately, or pleasing the Arab world and India (which held the oil and resources and strategic bases) and stopping any more Jews entering. With Britain weak at the end of the war, it wanted to avoid foreign conflict where possible and also disliked the prospect of being caught between a Palestinian uprising and Zionist terrorism.

This dilemma led it to set up deals between the opposing parties. If the U.S. would announce its willingness to allow vast numbers of Jews into the U.S., perhaps the Palestinians might accept the immediate entry of the 100,000. If the U.S. agreed not to press the Balfour Declaration and allow Palestine to quickly become a biracial state (with a Jewish province controlling its own immigration policy), the Arabs might agree to the entry of the 100,000. If the Jewish Agency agreed to disband the illegal Zionist armies in Palestine, perhaps the 100,000 could come in. Thus Britain attempted linkage.

The Labour Party resisted the U.S.'s frequent calls to let in 100,000 Jews immediately. Its arguments were: this would torpedo any hope of a future biracial state, it would violate the terms of the Balfour Declaration and the Mandate, and at least another division of British soldiers in Palestine, or U.S. help, would be required to impose such immigration on the hostile Palestinians.

Britain, as has been said, tried to keep distinct the two issues of Zionist immigration and rescue for European Jews. The emergency was attacked in a weak attempt to find temporary refuge or alternative havens for Jews. She had let into Britain (1938-39) a token 11,500 refugee children, 70% of them Jewish, and accepted some other Jewish refugees in the vain hope that the U.S. might open its own doors. She wanted the U.S. to realise that Palestine could not possible accept all Jewish refugees. The Foreign Office asked the Anglo-American Commission of Enquiry to "educate the Americans" and get them to act responsibly on the refugee question. Other countries, not only the U.S., could let in refugees as a special emergency procedure; UN member states should be encouraged to accept Jewish refugees. The Zionist argument that only Palestine could be a haven for the world's Jews was rejected. In fact, certain MPs (among them Paul Mason, supervising the refugee question for the Foreign Office) pointed out that it was almost anti-Semitic to argue that Jews could never by their nature be safe anywhere other than in Palestine. It was wrong and unrealistic to suggest that Palestine was their only possible haven.

Since the British quotas on immigration into Palestine still stood, the Zionists started on a programme of illegal immigration, with the Mossad le Aliyah Bet bringing in 1,000 Jews a month illegally just before the war and stepping up the numbers after the war ended. From the Istanbul headquarters Jews were moved from camps in the eastern zone to refugee camps in West Germany and Austria. By enormously increasing the number of Jewish refugees in the camps the Mossad hoped to make the U.S. exert pressure on Britain to let them into Palestine on humanitarian grounds. As David Ben Gurion said, "If we manage to concentrate a quarter of a million Jews in the U.S. zone it would increase the American pressure" (on Britain).[16] Between 1945-48, 250,000 East European Jews were transported to camps in the U.S. zone.

After the horrors of the Holocaust, the Zionists could and did portray Britain's unwillingness to save Jews as barbaric. When shiploads of immigrants were sent to Palestine, Britain could hardly return them to the refugee camps, so she put most of them in temporary camps in Cyprus and let them gradually into Palestine, against the quota numbers. But ships prevented from entering Palestine were given media coverage: the tragic 1940 Patria and 1942 Struma affairs were exploited to pressure Britain. In fact, from 1945 about 70,000 immigrants were run illegally to Palestine; 20,000 of them were allowed in.

As Norman Smith put it in the 1949 parliamentary debate:

> Faced by American wealth and Russian malice, we have not been able to prevent the illegal immigration which has been the Zionist weapon throughout.[17]

Britain's actions on immigration, therefore, were dictated by practical possibilities and calculations. We now turn to the U.S., where Jewish immigration into Palestine was differently handled.

Palestine was seen in the context of relieving Jews world-wide from discrimination, one form of discrimination being the ban on free movement; in 1911 the government abrogated its treaty with Russia because Russia was not allowing U.S. Jews into areas from which Jews were banned. Immigration into Palestine was seen as part of the Jews' right to move freely.

The U.S. approved both the Balfour Declaration and the Mandate, with their implications for immigration. The King-Crane Commission of 1919 alone recommended limiting immigration and abandoning the idea of a Jewish state. Apart from this, from

Woodrow Wilson on every president and from 1922 on every Congress supported Jewish immigration into Palestine.

Surprisingly, the American Jews were less united on the subject than the Christians. There was conflict as to whether the idea of a Jewish state were not blasphemous (forcing God's hand), a practical impossibility, a source of dual-loyalty problems, etc. But the ideological issue was obscured by other questions: should not individual Jews be allowed to go to Palestine if they so wished? Should they not be helped once there? This meant that Jews who disapproved of Zionism could nevertheless be co-opted into giving financial or other help to Jewish immigrants once in Palestine, and, later, saving them from the Holocaust.

The American Jewish Committee did not work for a Jewish homeland, of which it disapproved, but for a "haven." Other philanthropic Jews helped set up clinics, educational institutions etc. in Palestine. It was difficult to draw the line in practice between supporting a Jewish state (which many Jewish groups did not) and helping the Jewish community in Palestine (which in practice led on to the Zionist objective).

With the advent of Hitler, the need for a haven came to be seen as acute. From then on, interest in and commitment to rescue of European Jews expanded and membership of Jewish organisations went up from 50,000 (1938) to 150,000 (1942) to a million (1948). Sympathy for their persecuted brothers merged with a new way of looking at the Jewish problem, and a Jewish state started being promoted as an insurance policy for Jews world-wide. The question of immigration into Palestine, which had up to then been academic, became charged with emotional significance. The Zionists exploited the situation to the full, using pageants and rallies, lecture tours and articles in the media to publicise the fate of the European Jews.

The 1942 Biltmore Conference and the 1943 American Jewish Conference both called for unrestricted immigration into Palestine. The American Jewish Conference (incorrectly) presented itself to Americans as representative of all American Jewry and Jewish groups whose positions conflicted with the Conference's were accused of abandoning their brothers to their fate; in the current circumstances, few wished to be seen opposing moves to save Jews from almost certain death, and the Zionists used smear tactics to drive the point home. Many Jews who supported neither Zionism nor a Jewish state found themselves having to vote for resolutions calling for unlimited immigration into Palestine; others found that such resolutions were inextricably tacked onto other resolutions which they did want to support.

The Zionists also concentrated on propagandising American Christians. The Patria and Struma affairs were presented as tragedies where Jews preferred to die rather than not reach Palestine. Rabbis Wise and Silver whipped up anti-British feeling and constant propaganda efforts caused a rush to join movements in support of unlimited immigration. In 1941 the AFL called for more money to be sent to the "Jewish labouring masses" and for unrestricted immigration; the CIO joined it in attacking the White Paper, which was also criticised by then Senator Harry Truman as making "a scrap of paper out of Balfour's promise."[18]

Groups were set up to pressure Britain into repealing the White Paper: the American Palestine Committee, set up by Senators Wagner and McNary, demonstrated the sympathy of Christian America for the Jewish national home; 68 Senators and 200 Representatives joined. A Committee of Christian Leaders, Clergymen and Laymen on Behalf of Jewish Immigration into Palestine was formed. Where calls for outright Zionist aims might have been unsuccessful, in the years of Nazi persecution enormous sympathy for Jewish immigration into Palestine could be called up.

The administration, faced by both a "representative" Jewish body and Christian groups calling for unrestricted immigration, and without any corresponding group to put the Palestinian case, called loudly for Britain to let the Jews into Palestine.

Year by year attempts were made to force Britain to repeal the White Paper. The Congress passed resolutions to this effect in 1942 (63 Senators, 192 Representatives), 1943 (51 Senators and 194 Representatives), 1944 (411 out of 535 Congressmen) and 1945 (overwhelmingly, in both Houses). P.M. Attlee's offer to allow in 1,500 a month (which the Arabs had reluctantly accepted) was rejected by the Senate. In 1944 the state platforms of both parties called for unrestricted immigration and in presidential elections both candidates made multiple references to the issue, each outbidding the other: Truman's call for 100,000 to be let in was balanced by Dewey's to let in hundreds of thousands.

With Truman in power, pressure on Britain to repeal the White Paper was stepped up. President Truman had been a member of the national committee of the Campaign for a Jewish Army and was surrounded by Jewish friends and advisers. He was told that neglecting Zionist demands would harm his party's electoral chances whereas calls for immigration would enhance them. Truman, who had inherited rather than been elected to the presidency, was unsure of the level of popular support he enjoyed and was also aware that the Democratic Party was losing its traditional supporters. The Democrat Party's postmaster general, R.E. Hannegan, warned in 1946 that Thomas E. Dewey, the Republican candidate for president, intended to call for mass immigration and that Truman had better outbid him.

Funds as well as votes for the Democrat Party had to be attracted; the bargain was so evident that Defence Secretary John Forrestal declared that it was shameful that the U.S.'s foreign policy "was determined by the contributions a particular bloc of special interests might make to the party funds."[19]

No offers of financial help for dealing with the problems mass immigration would bring were forthcoming from the U.S. She was not interested in helping Britain or in compromises, in linking the numbers allowed in with some kind of political solution, or in offers that would let in less than the 100,000. Even the Anglo-American Committee report's attempt to link immigration with statehood found no support.

Truman persistently called on the British to let as many Jews into Palestine as possible, presenting Palestine as "their only hope of survival." Of the Anglo-American Committee report he approved only the part mentioning the entry of 100,000 Jews; he did not ratify the Anglo-American agreement and he rejected Britain's attempt in 1946 to make entry of the 100,000 conditional on Arab agreement.

Since the U.S. was risking neither money nor men in Palestine, and since the U.S. did not have significant amounts of government property there to protect, she could call for immigration with no fear of the consequences. While the Anglo-American Commission was still discussing the question and touring the Mideast, Dwight Eisenhower (reported Bartley C. Crum) was sending a military plane to Palestine, anticipating their decision, to judge whether or not the Jewish Agency were sufficiently well-prepared to handle the incoming 100,000!

Little attention was given to the search for other destinations for the Jews. Rhodesia, Kenya, Tanganyika, Cyrenaica, the Orinoco valley, Alaska and the Dominican Republic were considered briefly.

But, despite the conviction of the Anglo-American Committee that Palestine could not possibly host all European Jewish refugees, the one place large enough to have welcomed the Jews on a large scale—the U.S.—was not mentioned. While Britain, suffering bombardment and blockade, accepted a small number of European Jews, the U.S., so far from the war, so rich and with a history of welcoming immigrants, did not.

Neither the administration nor the Jewish groups nor Americans generally wanted the Jews to enter the U.S. Nativism and depression in the 1930s had caused a rise in anti-Semitism. A 1938-41 survey found that between one third and one half of the American people felt the Jews had too much power socially, economically and politically in the U.S. Baptist Gerald B. Winrod spoke of an international, Jewish financial conspiracy leading to the Depression. Father Charles E. Coughlin in his radio programmes blamed the Jews, as both capitalists and communists (!), for the Depression and for involving the U.S. in the war with Nazi Germany. Charles A. Lindbergh's Des Moines speech also charged the Jews, along with Britain and Roosevelt, with dragging America into war.

In 1945 a poll showed that only 5% of those polled wanted more immigrants let in. Societies such as the American Legion, the American Coalition of Patriotic Societies, the Veterans of Foreign Wars and the Daughters of the American Revolution, with millions of members, insisted on excluding further immigrants. Senator H. Burton expressed the view of most Americans when he said there were "many other places in the world where there is much more room for their reception than there is here."[20]

There was instead an attempt to cut the numbers allowed in. The 1939 Wagner-Rogers bill proposing to let 20,000 under-14-year-olds into the U.S. was rejected by Congress and hundreds of bills to cut immigration were presented. Procedural delay was intentionally rife, too, as Treasury lawyers admitted. All in all, during the war years, 10% of the possible quota of European Jews entered the U.S. The first year Truman called for 100,000 to enter Palestine (1945), 4,705 Jews entered the U.S. Only in 1948 was the immigration law changed.

Britain was not blind to the fact that the U.S., while urging Britain to open up Palestine, was unwilling to open its own doors. The Labour Government virtually accused the American administration of hypocrisy. Bevin said in 1946 that America's request would have been more impressive had she herself opened her doors wider to Hitler's victims. At the Labour Conference that year, he said Truman wanted 100,000 Jews to go to Palestine because he "did not want too many Jews in New York,"[21] and even pro-Zionist R. Crossman agreed that America's calls were designed to divert attention from the fact that her own immigration laws were one of the causes of the problem.

Other countries than Palestine could have provided refuge of at least a temporary kind. In 1944 the War Refugees Board was set up to help Jews to certain destinations in Canada, Sweden, Latin America and Britain and some 20,000 were got out of Europe. The State Department (which did not want to embarrass Britain) and the Zionists (it would impair the urgency of their claim to Palestine) opposed this solution.

The programme would anyway have needed money (the government gave a meagre sum) and the support of the American Jewish community (which was not forthcoming). Some Jewish groups gave help and money but the Zionists were totally opposed and managed to eliminate support: the Joint Emergency Committee on European Jewish Affairs, composed of various Jewish groups, was dissolved by Rabbi S.S. Wise and the American Jewish Congress.

The Emergency Conference to Save the Jewish People of Europe, with wide backing from the Roosevelts, Treasury and Foreign Affairs officials, the press under W.R. Hearst and non-Zionist Jewish groups, called for a government rescue agency but was opposed by the State Department and the Zionists for the reasons stated above.

The Bermuda Conference of 1943 talked and did nothing. Proposals were made to encourage European countries to welcome refugees, Jewish and non-Jewish alike. Its report was kept secret; nothing was done. Jacob Rosenheim of the Agudath Israel World Organisation saw its failure as the seal of doom for the European Jews: "The Bermuda Conference has crushed any chance of hope for the rescue of our unhappy brethren and sisters doomed to death by Hitler."[22] But the Zionist Chairman of the House Foreign Affairs Committee, Jewish Congressman Sol Bloom, declared himself "as a Jew [I am] perfectly satisfied with the results."[23] The Zionists were pushing Palestine as the only possible refuge and were prepared to use European Jews as pawns; the administration was convinced that representative Jews did not want to save European Jewry elsewhere.

The attitude of the seven Jewish Congressmen illustrates their desire to call for a Zionist solution rather than rescue Jews. Only Emmanuel Celler pressed for rescue. Of the Jews surrounding Roosevelt (Niles, Baruch, Lehman, Frankfurter and Rosenman) none called for rescue. Only anti-Zionist groups suggested opening America's doors. The Zionists' attitude to rescue shocked and surprised many. Senator Gillette expressed dismay at their tactics, and when Morris Ernst was sent by Roosevelt to travel the west and see which nations would accept immigrants, he was astounded to find himself not welcomed but vituperatively attacked by the Zionists. The programme of returning Jews to their places of origin along with other refugees, begun in 1945, was criticised by the Zionists. They implied that only in Palestine could Jews be safe and tried to torpedo all other rescue possibilities.

This ploy was recognised by General Frederick Morgan, who worked in the refugee camps as an UNRRA official. He realised that Jews were being sent by the Zionists to Palestine via Italy and Yugoslavia after being trained and organised in the camps. He said many would have preferred to go to the U.S. For this he was denounced as anti-Semitic and a reincarnation of Adolph Hitler by Eddie Cantor in *The New York Times* and was sacked from his post by the two (Zionist) directors general of UNRRA, R. Lehman, governor of New York State, and Fiorello La Guardia, mayor of New York City.

British MPs who visited the camps held the same view: R. Crossman said that of course there had been Zionist propaganda in the camps and that his group had bitterly opposed Jews going anywhere other than Palestine; Norman Smith reported that he had found that Jews with some English had told him they wished to go to the U.S. "But the Zionists had arranged otherwise," he said, while America's remained static.[24] But the result was that, by the time Britain had ceased imposing Jewish immigration on the Palestinian Arabs, the immigrants were sufficiently numerous and sufficiently well-armed to be able to fend for themselves.

We therefore turn now to the question of arms and terror.

Here too Britain responded to circumstance and the U.S. took a more emotional stance. During both World Wars and the Arab rebellion the Zionists offered their services to Britain and were given arms, training and funds. When Britain began to limit immigration and use of weapons, they turned to the U.S. for arms and the money with which to buy them.

Terror—"gun Zionism"—had been advocated since the start of the century by Jabotinsky and his followers, who saw a well-equipped force as a prerequisite for a Jewish State. Britain needed Zionist help in Palestine in the First World War and set up the short-lived Zionist Mule Corps and the Jewish Legion. To deal with the 1936-9 Palestine rebellion Britain trained 14,500 Jewish fighters as "supernumerary policemen" to work in collaboration with the Jewish Agency. (Article IV of the Mandate stipulated that Britain work with the Agency.) Britain ignored the Agency's links with terror groups and allowed an official military force to be paid and equipped. In fact, the Jewish Settlement Police included a large number of Haganah members and this gave Haganah a semi-legal existence. A Special Night Squad was set up under (Zionist) Colonel Orde Wingate and brilliantly trained for use against the Palestinians. After publication of the White Paper, David Ben Gurion prepared to use force against Britain, with help from the U.S.

World War II presented the Zionists with an opportunity to fight Hitler alongside Britain and at the same time get permission to form a legal Jewish Army. As Weizmann pledged support for Britain, Neville Chamberlain and Anthony Eden agreed to organise this Jewish Army. There would be 10,000 Jews, 4,000 from Palestine; they would receive training in Britain and fight in the Middle East. Army and Colonial Office pressure stopped the plan until in 1944 Churchill created the 5,000-strong Jewish Army, fighting under the Star of David. So a small Jewish Army got legitimacy, training and arms and a hope of a share in the post-war carve-up.

Britain also permitted military operations in Palestine. In 1940 an agreement was made with the Jewish Agency that Britain would allow Jewish operations (even if these were officially banned by the Mandate) and would pay and equip Jewish Agency and Haganah forces while on British expeditions. The Haganah set up special commando units and an intelligence service and Britain enabled it to double in size from 36,900 men (1944) to 70,000 (1946).

As for arms, the war proved a godsend for the Zionists. Haganah acquired arms legally from Britain and from Vichy French forces in Syria. It stole supplies from British stores in Palestine. It got pickings from the battlefields. At the end of the war it got arms from Italy, France, Yugoslavia, Poland, Czechoslovakia, the USSR and the U.S. It also manufactured its own arms and had contracts with the British Army, supplying Britain in 1942-4 with $33 million of equipment. Under the Mandate it produced bombs, machine guns, anti-tank mines, small arms, naval craft etc. and recruited, strengthened kibbutz fortifications and grew in size and power. By the mid-1940s it was so powerful that British General J.C. D'Arcy, commander of the British forces in Palestine, thought it could hold Palestine "against the entire Arab world"[25] and R. Crossman agreed in 1946 that Haganah was "the most powerful force in the Middle East, apart from the British Army."[26]

Terror groups also existed, loosely linked to Haganah and the Jewish Agency—the Irgun Zvei Leumi (IZL) and the LEHI, its offshoot. Irgun used terror first against the Palestinians and after the White Paper against Britain. Although its high command was arrested it continued to function. It established contacts with fascist Italy in 1940 and with Nazi Germany in 1941 and later with the USSR. It suspended operations during the war though "We still thought of the British as the enemy," as Stern Gang Yaacov Avneri later said, referring back to 1939.[27] LEHI, or the Stern Gang, was a breakaway group, led in 1943-46 by Yitzhak Shamir, using indiscriminate terror against Palestinians and British.

Britain had not envisaged arming terror groups against British soldiers. Orde Wingate was suspected of helping the Zionists against Britain and was banned from Palestine. He told his Special Night Squad friends, when he knew the order was coming for his removal, that the British government and the military in Palestine "want to hurt me and you."[28]

Britain was never sure how far the Jewish Agency was implicated in terror activity. When in 1946 the Agency took part in combined operations with LEHI, the IZL and Haganah, it insisted that it could not discipline terrorist elements. Britain, having to work with the Agency, wished to believe its protestations of innocence. A Colonial Secretary report in 1946 accusing the Agency of conniving at terrorist activity was shelved by the Cabinet, which decided not to search for arms or pressure the Agency. The Agency publicly condemned terror acts against the British.

Britain was thus caught between working with the Agency and suspecting it of fomenting trouble. When five officers were kidnapped, the Agency was finally searched, its office occupied, some of its Executive and 2,688 of its members arrested and 700 put in camps and told it must not be a cover for terrorism. There was much criticism of this in the British Government, where the Agency's innocence was still believed. And in November 1947, when the Agency dissociated itself from terror, its members were let out of the camps again. Since Britain found it hard to check the Agency there was an attempt to cajole it and get it to discipline its members itself. Aneurin Bevan in January 1947 suggested that if the Agency co-operated in putting down terror, immigration might be increased. This was not a successful tactic.

The Zionists attacked British property, causing an estimated £4 million damage in 1946 (explosions in government offices, radio stations, bridges and the King David Hotel, military camps raided, two sergeants hanged and booby-trapped, etc.). Between £30 to £40 million a year was spent, Churchill reckoned, in policing. The Chancellor of the Exchequer, Sir Stafford Cripps, believed that between January 1945 and December 1947 £100 million had been spent containing Jewish violence in Palestine. Britain had just come out of an expensive war; this further drain on her resources prompted her to feel that either she needed a Zionist promise to disarm or she would hand the problem over to the UN.

Trying the first policy first, P.M. Clement Attlee called on Jewish and Arab groups to disband, tried to link a future increase in immigration to the disarming of illegal armies, asked the Jewish Agency to co-operate, asked the U.S. to stop funding terror—all in vain. Arresting terror leaders only alienated the U.S., whose financial help Britain badly needed. The U.S. refused to contribute money or men to help Britain keep order. So the second alternative was finally tried and Britain handed over to the UN.

The U.S.'s attitude to Zionist terror was totally different. She had had no practical reasons for courting Jewish help in the two World Wars or against a Palestinian rebellion. She did not have soldiers in Palestine and was not spending American money there. She could therefore feel free from any practical considerations and view the issue from within her own terms of reference.

Within these terms, the British were seen as imperialists and the Jewish fighters as a modern equivalent of the Boston patriots. This view was backed up by the Zionists, who had presented the idea of a Jewish Army to Britain in practical terms of usefulness, but presented the concept to the Americans in moral, ethical terms.

Thus: Jews could only be rescued in Palestine, and to hold Palestine force was necessary; Britain was preventing Jews being saved in Palestine and could therefore with moral justice be attacked.

There was public interest in the idea of a Jewish Army. In 1943 one-third of the Senate backed it, along with 1,500 signatories, ex-President Herbert Hoover, Eleanor Roosevelt, Fiorello La Guardia, W.R. Hearst and Harry Truman, who was a member of its national committee.

Money was sent to the Army. David Ben Gurion stated, "We got many millions of dollars from the United States."[29] American Friends of a Jewish Palestine, a Jabotinsky-influenced group with clandestinely-operating Irgun members, sent money, as did the Friends of the Haganah Inc.; the Jewish Appeal sent $35 million in 1945 and the Jewish Agency in America $3-1/2 million in 1946. Front-line organisations such as the Sonnenborn Institute gave money. Golda Myerson (later Meir) raised $50 million on a short visit to the States. Jewish groups and philanthropists sent money and so did the Jewish underworld and its rich Mafia friends.

In 1946 Haganah sent emissaries to the U.S. to raise cash for arms and contacted the Jewish gangster milieu. In all, millions of dollars were collected from gangsters such as Bugsy Siegel, Dutch Shultz, Abner Zwillman, Mickey Cohen, Moe Dalitz, etc. and their Mafia counterparts. The Jewish underworld could supply arms and money and get them run into Palestine. Sam May, for example, was friendly with the President of Panama and got arms sent in Panamanian ships. As "Ruben," a Haganah representative in the U.S., said, "All our ships carrying weapons to Israel were registered in Panama and flew under the Panamanian flag. This was a very, very great help to us."[30] Meyer Lansky's Mafia associates controlled the New York and New Jersey docks and sent military hardware shipments direct to Palestine.

All in all, American Jewish aid to the Zionists amounted to about $275 million over the period 1943-48. (One of the main aims of the 1948 British Prevention of Terror Ordinance was to stop American dollars reaching the terrorist organisations.)

By 1947, the State Department had made it illegal to sell arms to combatants in Palestine. But arms continued to reach Palestine. And this expressed a commonly-felt wish: by February 1948, a hundred thousand telegrams and letters had poured in to the White House calling for arms to be sent to Haganah. Whether these letters were genuine or not, the administration could permissibly feel that the sympathy of the country was with the Zionists.

As for the question of whether the Jewish Agency should not be held responsible for terror operations, this the Zionists resolved neatly. Golda Myerson, then temporary head of the Agency's political department, told the Americans that it was practically impossible for the Agency to take on police tasks, controlling terror, without the apparatus of a state to do the job!

The press encouraged the American public to side with the Zionists against the British. Rabbi B. Korff wrote in the New York Post that not giving aid to Haganah was anti-Semitic! Ben Hecht, a Hollywood script-writer and correspondent for the New York *Herald Tribune*, wrote 15 May 1947 of the jubilation felt whenever terror worked against the British. "Every time you blow up a British arsenal, or wreck a British jail, or send a British rail-road sky-high, or rob a British bank, or let go with your guns and bombs at the British betrayers and invaders of your homeland, the Jews of America make a little holiday in their hearts."[31]

British protests, asking how Americans would feel if British Communists rejoiced publicly whenever the U.S. was harmed, were ignored by the administration. This was not surprising: Truman's attitude to the Jewish terrorists imprisoned by Britain in 1946 had been clear—he wrote to Attlee hoping that they would soon be released!

Possibly the administration was already committed to establishing links with the intelligence branch of the Zionist network. In wartime Italy, where the Zionists were smuggling arms and men into Palestine, friendly relations were being set up with them by Office of Strategic Studies agent James Jesus Angleton, later to become a top CIA man with Mossad links.

Britain's attempts to get the Americans to take a more responsible position on terror were rejected. Her suggestions that the U.S. put men and money into implementing the resolutions of the Anglo-American Committee were turned down. Her hope that the U.S. would help implement the partition plan was dashed. The U.S. did not want to be sucked into fighting against the Zionists. Its policy was to call for a Jewish haven in Palestine; if this haven needed arms and terror to be set up, so be it.

The third context in which we should view Britain's and the U.S.'s attitudes to immigration and a Jewish Army is that of the popular perception of the issues.

The ways in which the British and Americans articulated their ideas on immigration and a Jewish Army illustrate their different sympathies and reasonings. The arguments used in the two countries to justify their policies in Palestine show to what extent they saw the problem in a similar way (the right of a more advanced group to dominate a native, less advanced group; the desire to set up a perfect socialist community) and to what extent their views and identifications differed (idea of a Chosen People, occupying a land by divine right; idea of a repressed people involved in an independence struggle against a repressive mother country).

The arguments that are used to justify policies are important; they are those which are likely to be persuasive. If the Zionists used various arguments in Britain and others in the U.S., it was precisely because they clearly recognised that the idea of the Chosen People had enormous resonance in the U.S. and hardly any in Britain and that foreign policy calculations interested the British government more than any other.

Also, arguments help form policy. Policy can only be made within a framework of accepted assumptions. These automatic assumptions were different in Britain and the U.S.

Lastly, in the U.S. the people had influence over what the administration did to a far greater extent than in Britain. So ideas deeply held by the people would be taken into consideration by an administration and passionately held convictions would give the context in which an administration could operate.

By order of frequency of reference, in Britain debate on the Palestine issue concentrated mainly on calculating which activity would best help British interests abroad, then on deciding whether the policy under consideration conformed to the Balfour Declaration, then on the rights of a modernising race to occupy an undeveloped land, then on the desirability of introducing the first socialist experiment to take place in a new nation. In the U.S., debate turned on the right of the Jews to occupy a land given by God to them for all eternity, then on a desire to compensate for the European Holocaust and prevent it ever happening again, then on consistency to the U.S.'s traditional policy of support for the idea of a Jewish state.

British criticism of America's stance was that the U.S. was subject to the Zionist vote and influence, that she could only see one side of the question, that she was calling for policy which she had no intention of helping to implement and that she was encouraging terror. The U.S. accused Britain of being swayed by imperialist wishes and the desire to remain on good terms with the Arabs, of abandoning a firm promise given in the Balfour Declaration and of repressing a colonised people fighting for independence (the Zionists, not the Arabs). Each people brought to the issues its own perceptions and assumptions, formed by its own history and worldview.

The first, emotive, line of thought in the U.S. was that the Jews had a God-given right to Palestine. This idea was almost entirely lacking in British debate. Where British Zionists like Churchill admired the Jews for their long history—"The coming into being of a Jewish State in Palestine is an event in world history to be viewed in the perspective, not of a generation or a century, but in the perspective of a thousand or two thousand or even three thousand years...This is an event in world history"[32]—there were no references to God's plan for the Jews' return or His watchful care for His Chosen People.

But in America it was different. For the fundamentalists, who believed in the literal truth of every word of the Bible, there was written proof that God had bestowed, for eternity, Palestine upon the Israelites and, secondly, that part of His divine plan was the regathering of the Jews in Palestine as a prelude to the Second Coming of Jesus Christ.

References were multiple. Genesis 17, 8 says, "I will give unto thee and to thy seed unto thee, the land wherein thou art a stranger, all the land of Canaan, for an everlasting possession." (Genesis 15, 18 bequeaths the area between the Nile and the Euphrates.) Other texts give the Israelites the right to drive out the original inhabitants of the land (Deuteronomy 4, 38: "To drive out nations from before thee greater and mightier than thou art, to bring thee in, to give thee their land for an inheritance.").

These texts, plus Deuteronomy 5, 2, and Leviticus 26, 42 and 45, and, generally, the first three books of the Bible, give the Israelites divine sanction to take Palestine. It was strongly believed that this promise was just as binding in the 20th century as it had been when the Bible was written; it was not a promise limited in time but written for eternity. Immigration into Palestine and the use of force to remain there was therefore not only permitted to the Jews but an obligation on them, according to the fundamentalists.

To fundamentalist Americans—and Protestant America in the 1920s and 30s witnessed a great upsurge of fundamentalism—the words of the Bible were the exact words of God. Their meaning was not metaphorical and the Bible was not a text of anthropological interest. The meaning was clear. The Jews were entitled to this particular piece of real estate.

The next element of religious sanction for a Jewish state lay in the belief that God had promised to restore the Jews, who had been driven out of their land. His promise to re-gather the Jews was associated with a promise that this would introduce the Second Coming. One text to prove this was Matthew 24, 20: "Pray that your flight be not in the winter, neither on the sabbath day." (At the end of the world, the Jews would be observing the sabbath and therefore logically in a country where this sabbath would be enforced, i.e., a Jewish state.) Another text was Ezekiel 38, 8: "In the latter years thou shalt come into the land that is brought back from the sword...it is brought forth out of the nations." (The Israelites return from their diaspora and take the land by force of arms.) Ezekiel 39, 27-8 repeats: "I have gathered them unto their own land...then shall they know that I am the Lord their God." (After being re-gathered in Israel, the Jews will convert to Christianity.) Zechariah 12, 10 tells how the Israelites will be in Palestine, Jesus will return to the Mount of Olives, "they shall look upon me whom they have pierced" and then "the Lord my God shall come, and all the saints with thee." Luke 21, 24 anticipates the end of non-Jewish rule over Jerusalem.

These and other Bible texts were viewed by fundamentalists as giving the Jews a divinely-backed right to Palestine. Also, texts showed that Christians had to support this effort: "I will bless them that bless thee, and curse them that curseth thee" (Genesis 12, 3).

All Adventist groups wanted the Second Coming to be in their own lifetime. If restoring the Jews to Palestine would speed on the return of Jesus and the coming millennium then it was a Christian's duty to help the Jews back to Palestine as quickly as possible.

Not only Bible texts referred to the Jews' eventual return to their land; Mormon texts were far more explicit.

The Book of Mormon speaks of the fate of the Jews and of their eventual return to Palestine, helped *by the United States*. Nephi 2, 3, 13 speaks of "restoring thee, O house of Israel." Nephi 3, 20, 28 quotes God: "I have covenanted with them that I would gather them together in mine own due time, that I would give unto them again the land of their fathers for their inheritance, which is the Land of Jerusalem, which is the promised land unto them forever." Nephi 1, 22, 12 refers again to this idea of the Jews being brought out of captivity and gathered in the lands of their inheritance, after which they will convert to Christianity. There are further references in Nephi 1, 15, 19 to the "restoration of the Jews in the latter days" as well as in Esther 13, 5.

The prophecies in the Book of Mormon foretell the coming of a mighty Gentile nation in America (the U.S.) which will eventually carry the Jews back to Palestine: "Through the fullness of the Gentiles, the remnant of their seed, who shall be scattered forth upon the face of the earth because of their unbelief, shall be brought in" (Nephi 3, 16, 4).

Even though mainline Christians did not interpret the Scriptures so literally, there was a large body of Christians who did believe in divine sanction for the restoration of the Jews to Palestine.

These themes continually appear in American politicians' references. The idea of the Jews being restored, re-gathered, and rehabilitated appears constantly, unlike in Britain. This serves two purposes: it gives divine legitimacy to the Zionist venture, and it implies a correction, a rectifying, of a wrong a return to a former, right, condition. Thus nothing new or debatable is to be attempted; a wrong is to be righted.

Examples can be found in the speeches of many American figures. John Adams said in 1818 that he wished the Jews "again in Judea an independent nation" and in 1848 President John Quincy Adams called for the Jews to return to their homeland. President Woodrow Wilson expressed his feeling of humble awe that he might have a part to play in the working out of divine destiny: "To think that I the son of the manse should be able to restore the Holy Land to its people," he remarked.[33] President W.G. Harding spoke of the "restoration" of Palestine to the Jews and H. Hoover of the "rehabilitation of Palestine as a true homeland."

In 1941 Senators Wagner's and McNary's American Palestine Committee, with strong Congressional support, spoke of re-establishing the Jewish national home and in 1945 Congress said the Jewish state had to be rebuilt. Even the Communist Party of America spoke of "rebuilding" the Jewish homeland.

The Zionists made much of this concept. The American Zionist Emergency Council issued a booklet in 1944 specifically entitled:

"The Attitude of Official America and of the American People Toward the Rebuilding of Palestine as a Free and Democratic Jewish Commonwealth."

This constant use of the prefix "re" was never used by British MPs. For the British, the terms of reference for the Jewish issue were entirely secular. Fundamentalism was not part of the British 20th century mind-set. A mild Anglicanism or secularism was more usual.

Indeed, the only mention of a religious element in justifying a Jewish return to Palestine was a scornful comment by Norman Smith in the January 1949 House of Commons debate. He asked rhetorically, "What is Zionism but the expressed belief of certain fanatical Jews that they are the Chosen People, who ought to have a national State in Palestine, a country which they left 20 centuries ago?"[34] He added a dry comment that this belief was backed up in the U.S. by big money. The idea of the Jews returning to Palestine as part of God's plan seemed worthy only of ridicule.

This emotional conviction that the Jews should return to Palestine was underlined in the U.S. with an emotional identification. The Americans saw themselves as a Chosen People like the other Chosen People. This brought them to feel strong sympathy with the Zionists and gave them a corresponding lack of interest in the Arabs' plight.

From the time of the first settlers in America there had been a conscious identification of the Americans with the Israelites. The Americans perceived themselves as an elect, a chosen, race. The parallels between their history and that of the Israelites was, they thought, striking. Edward Johnson entitled his account of New England's early days "The Wonder Working Providence of Zion's Saviour in New England." He saw the Puritans as God's soldiers. Americans saw themselves as having fled a corrupt regime (Egypt-Britain) which had stubbornly refused to covenant with God; they had had a trying journey (Sinai-Atlantic) to set up a city on a hill (Jerusalem-The New Jerusalem). They, the elect, among all the world, were to be saved and their very sense of having been chosen by God, along with the rules they set for governing their society, proved that they were among the chosen. The success of their society proved God was with them; failure would be a sign that they were not the elect but the damned. Their enemies, like the Israelites', were all around them—the hostile Indians and the ungodly nations of Europe—and within, and both were to be vanquished.

Such ideas were clearly stated and applied in the first colonies. In 1607 Virginia covenanted to build the New Jerusalem and apply strict Old Testament law (the arrival of large numbers of non-Puritans later made this an impossibility). The Plymouth colony viewed the situation thus: the Lord had saved them from a storm at sea and they had written out a covenant defining their future relationship with God; from 1629 the colony strictly adhered to the terms of this covenant. John Winthrop stated clearly: "We are entered into a covenant."[35] The short-lived New Haven colony wrote out the strictest covenant of all.

There was certainly comfort for new colonists, faced with an unknown land and physical danger, to know that God was on their side. This advantage could not be risked. The bargain was that God would protect them and they would implement His will with all possible strictness. The colonists regulated all aspects of their life according to the terms of that other covenant they knew—that of God and the Israelites. The Old Testament dictated the terms of their own covenant and they followed as closely as possible ancient Israelite habits of dress, obedience to parents (disobedience punishable by death), naming (use of Old Testament names), sabbath observance instead of Sunday holiday, compulsory church attendance enforced by the militia, justice (scripture cited rather than common law; in New Haven no trial by jury), weights and measures in New Haven, personal behaviour and government (by church members only, with tests to make sure each leader was "elect"), backed up with severe punishment for offenders. The "blue laws" covered every aspect of life.

There were sufficient Bible stories of how God had encouraged the Israelites to fight off other groups by deceitful means to allow the colonists to permit themselves great latitude in repulsing the native Indians. They could cheat, break treaties and massacre in the knowledge that the Israelites, too, had done this with God's blessing—it was part of the covenant. Colonists interpreted victories in this manner: Captain John Mason, besieging an Indian fort where hundreds of Indians were slaughtered by his men, said God had "laughed his enemies and the enemies of his people to scorn."[36]

Enemies also included critics inside the colonies. No tolerance of religious deviation was possible; exclusion was the only way of protecting the colony from harmful elements which might encourage God to stop protecting the settlement. Roger Williams and Anne Hutchinson had to be driven out; Mary Dyer, who kept trying to return, was hanged in 1660. The militia were used against Samuel Gorton and his followers.

Keeping the covenant guaranteed success; success the Americans had. Though the original fervour died, the idea that God was especially interested in America persisted. By the time of the independence war (which again proved that God was helping America) about 85% of the churches still held to this covenant idea and the blue laws were still in force. The discussions about the seal of the newly-independent nation show how minds were still focused on this Biblical perception of themselves and their world: Benjamin Franklin's suggestion showed Moses and Pharaoh and the drowning of the Egyptians, Thomas Jefferson's the Israelites being led by a pillar of fire by night and cloud by day. The Americans were the latter-day Israelites.

This perception continued into the 19th and 20th centuries. Writer Herman Melville saw the Americans as the "peculiar, chosen people, the Israelites of our time."[37] God's blessing covered massacring Indians even when they were no longer a real threat. Methodist Colonel Chevington was a typical Bible-bearing soldier, declaring that he had come to kill Indians.

Politicians' statements were consistent as to America's special role. Senator Beveridge said the U.S. was trustee, under God, of the civilisation of the world; President McKinley that she was His chosen nation, to lead in the regeneration of the world. President Woodrow Wilson believed that America was born to exemplify a devotion to Biblical righteousness. (Later in the century, President Ronald Reagan was to make numerous references to America's relationship with God, who was "always in this divine scheme of things keeping his eye on our land, guiding it as a promised land for these people."[38])

The Mormons also saw the U.S. as a promised land. The Book of Mormon described how the ten lost Israelite tribes had wandered thither and had degenerated into the Indians. Jesus Christ had appeared in America. The colonists were to emigrate from a corrupt country to re-establish the correct faith in the U.S. after which, a proud and righteous people, they would set up a godly nation in the promised land (of America) and gather the Jews together (in

Palestine). The Mormons saw the Declaration of Independence and the Constitution as divinely inspired and expected other, future, prophecies for the U.S.

Thus, to the Zionists Palestine and to the Americans the U.S. was central to God's plan. Identification was easy. And as the Israelites had in the past defeated Moabites, Canaanites, Philistines, etc. and the Americans had defeated Indians and colonial powers, so now it was permissible for the Zionists to defeat the Arabs. Immigration and the force of arms were common themes in the destinies of the two groups.

The British completely lacked this sense of being a chosen people, protected by God, with a god-given right to deprive the original inhabitants of their land. For a thousand years the British had not seen themselves as immigrants.

Where the Americans lacked any sense of the rights of the original inhabitants to a land, the British could identify and sympathise with this feeling for land. They had inhabited the same small piece of territory for over a thousand years and had built up a relationship with this village, that field, this farmyard which the pioneering Americans could not. They could understand that the Palestinians wanted that land and no other. When they tried to balance claims (Jewish and Arab) to the land, they tried to find a solution on that land, whereas the Americans wondered where the Palestinians could be moved to (like the Indians); this explains American suggestions to move them to, for example, Jordan or Iraq. Where the Americans "saw" the Palestinians, they only saw them as a hindrance to the Zionists; where the British "saw" them, they recognised the rights that two thousand years of possession could bring. As civil servant Freya Stark put it: "The habitation of a land for two thousand years gives one a right to close or open the door."[39]

Bevin pointed this out clearly in his 1949 speech to Parliament:

> We understand how this strikes the Arabs—all the Arab people, not only their Governments—and we should consider how the British people would have reacted if a similar demand had been made on us. Suppose we had been asked to give up a slice of Scotland, Wales or Cornwall to another race, and that the present inhabitants had been compelled to make way. I think there would have been trouble in this House and possibly outside.[40]

Another way of perceiving the issue, however, was more or less shared by British and Americans. This was the belief that it was in the interests of the world (and even of a less "advanced" civilisation) that a "superior" civilisation replace an inferior one. As Arab League Secretary General Abdul Rahman Azzam had pointed out, this belief was one that every colonising power had held and made into an excuse for colonising; a "backward" race had to be pulled "forward." The backward race here was what U.S. Clark Clifford termed "a few nomadic desert tribes!"

Britain and the U.S. had a history of "helping civilisation on" and both waxed lyrical as to what the Zionists could achieve in Palestine. Pro-Zionists in Britain used this as a major argument, whereas in the U.S. it was less frequently stated.

Winston Churchill, approving a hydro-electric concession for the Zionists in 1922, stated his position:

> Left to themselves, the Arabs of Palestine would not in a thousand years have taken effective steps toward the irrigation and electrification of Palestine. They would have been quite content to dwell—a handful of philosophic people—in the wasted sun-scorched plains, letting the waters of the Jordan continue to flow unbridled and unharnessed into the Dead Sea.[41]

In the January 1949 debate he spoke of the contrasting effects Arab and Jewish occupation of the land had: "One has only to look up to the hills that once were cultivated and then were defaced by centuries of medieval barbarism, to see what has been accomplished" with Jewish immigration. The Jews were an efficient race: "Their efforts are amazing—to bring back into economic usefulness lands which the world cannot afford to leave lying idle." And, "The Jews, by the gift they have and the means they do not lack, have a way of making the desert bloom.... The Arabs, for all their dignity and grace, are primarily the children of the desert...and for the most part, the desert lands do not become reclaimed while the Arab control is complete over them."[42]

There could hardly be a more revealing illustration of the mind-set of the British pro-Zionist. Ignoring everything the Palestinians had achieved, there was a concentration on what the (European) Jews would bring—European, for the Sephardic, oriental Jews who already lived in Palestine were classed with the Arabs. Then this coming modernisation was made to justify possession of the land.

Modernising, as Balfour stated, was of "far profounder import than the desires and prejudices of the 700,000 Arabs who now inhabit that ancient land."[43]

R. Crossland echoed the view that the tide of progress must not be stemmed, deserts must not be kept deserted, etc. But there seems to have been a willful unwillingness to look at what precisely the situation in Palestine was: was it an underdeveloped wilderness? What about the towns, cities, local governments of Palestine? In his view, "these villages were only mud huts anyhow. They were terribly bad villages full of vermin."[44] That was his Palestinian reality.

British non-Zionists countered these arguments by pointing out that Palestinians were not so very backward and that the Zionists who were referred to were all European and none of them oriental Jews, and thus could be seen as colonisers. As A. Crawley said, the Zionists were "in character and civilisation as alien both to the Arabs in Palestine and to the original Jewish inhabitants as any other European or Western race would have been,"[45] and other MPs noted the analogy with the French settlers in Algeria. Back in 1909 A. Aaronsohn had compared Jewish colonisation in Palestine to that of the French in Tunisia. This the Americans never recognised, though certain British MPs and Abdul Rahman Azzam pointed it out.

Then the British non-Zionists put forward the argument that even if there was an anticipated advance of civilisation, this could not justify forcing the original inhabitants off the land. Freya Stark wrote, "We have heard a little too much from herren-people who come on the plea of superior efficiency" (the Nazis) to allow efficiency to permit a take-over of land on that pretext. She also argued that the modernising effect of the Zionists had more to do with money than some innate Jewish characteristic, as Churchill had implied. She compared what the Palestinians were doing, with their sparse resources, with what the Zionists could do with " the riches of Zionism, drawn from all the world: it is rather like David and Goliath, the other way round."[46] She would have concurred with Abdul Rahman Azzam that, given money and education, any country could modernise within fifteen years. That removed a major part of the "civilisational" Zionist argument.

Though the Americans assumed that the "advanced" had the right to replace the "less advanced," they made far fewer references to this than the British Zionists. And even after the Arab riots had convinced the British that the Palestinians did not see themselves in the light of beneficiaries, the Americans could not adapt their approach to this new perception, with the American members of the Anglo-American Committee still referring to how Jewish development would benefit the Arabs. And the Zionists, leaving nothing to chance, tried to underline the Americans' perception of both themselves and the Zionists as people representing the advance of modernism over a more primitive people. When the Anglo-American Committee was in Palestine, Supreme Court judge (and Zionist) Felix Frankfurter advised the Zionists to take the visiting Americans to see the new-born Jews in the new settlements; this, he said, would remind them of the Far West pioneers and America's own heritage. It would once again identify Americans with Zionists.

An idea linked to that of advancing civilisation was one of advancing civilisation of a particular kind—socialist. Both Americans and British shared the view that a Jewish Palestine was likely to advance the cause of socialism by putting it into practice in virgin territory. Much was made of Zionist communal swamp-draining and kibbutz life, demonstrating that it was a realisation of Aaron David Gordon's idea of the "conquest of labour" and had an intrinsic moral value. Much was made too of the Histadrut and its pivotal place in society. The American unions (AFL, CIO and the smaller United Hebrew Trades, ILGWU, Amalgamated Clothing and Jewish Labor Committee) saw a modern western socialist ideal being put into practice. So did the British Labour Party. Norman Smith spoke of how the Zionists had appealed to the trade unions' feelings and had lured them into supporting Zionism thus. R. Crossman referred to the 3,900 Jewish Haganah leaders arrested by the British as "for the most part good sound trade unionists."[47] But where the American union movement continued to believe in the socialism and humanity of Zionism, the British movement split, with some unionists feeling that they had been deluded.

The last major theme perceived by British and Americans was the most divisive. The British saw themselves as having obligations to the Palestinians as well as to the Jews (rather as they had in the 1750s and 60s felt an obligation to protect the Indians against the colonists) whereas the Americans saw the Zionists as 20th century freedom fighters striving against a repressive imperialism. The British saw their purpose as fighting a Jewish Army which was becoming uncontrollable and the Americans saw theirs as supporting a people's army (like their own 18th century militias) against a tyrannical standing army (as in the War of Independence).

Obviously, in Britain there were few who could defend an army fighting against' Britain's own, particularly when the British Army was on the receiving end of such terror tactics as booby-trapping of soldiers. There was frustration, too, at having to work with the Jewish Agency while, as Attlee said, the Agency seemed to be acting as a cover for running an illegal army involved in illegal activities. The British recognised how the Zionists were manipulating propaganda effects (the Patria and Struma affairs, the political use of the refugee camps) and realized how much Zionist terror was costing them in men and money. They were exasperated at the Americans' continuing support for the Haganah and terror groups.

But the Americans, again, saw things from their own historical perspective and from within their sense of their own identity. The Americans idealised the Zionist army as a mirror image of their own 18th century militias, fighting off both Indians and the British professional army which tried to limit the American expansion. References were made to the Founding Fathers and, more specifically, to the Boston Tea Party. One group of Zionist volunteers was even called the George Washington Legion! Truman's adherence to the National Committee for a Jewish Army and all his attempts to protect arrested terrorists could be seen in this light. Such terror could never have been countenanced if used by any group inside the U.S. against the federal government, but the Zionists were seen through a different perception.

The British army had been in the 18th century a professional one, fighting for strategic and defined objectives, fighting according to the rules of war. But the American militias had resembled the Zionists' army in many ways: citizens were armed, like the Zionist settlers; they were not under professional rules (Washington had said his army was so undisciplined that he would have to send off half the army to find the other half!) but were half-farmers, half-fighters, like the Zionists; their tactics against Indians and British were daring and devious, as were the Zionists'; they had fought another race for land. Suspicions that Britain wanted to retain an imperial position in the Middle East were fuelled by folk-memories of Britain as the corrupt, ungodly empire that had "repressed" the Americans and many rejoiced to see Britain humiliated by a small settler community.

Britain was presented as being in a classic colonialist position, holding down with troops a people asking for its independent national home (the Jews, not the Palestinians!).

In this way the Americans read their own history into the Zionists' project in Palestine.

Thus, Britain's and America's policies on Jewish immigration and a Jewish Army can be examined within three main frameworks.

The first, the overall context of commitment to Zionism, shows Britain starting on a strong Zionist policy which was entered on for foreign policy reasons and then diluted for the same reasons. The Zionists said Britain had betrayed her commitment. The U.S.'s commitment to Zionism increased particularly after the Holocaust and after Ben Gurion had turned Zionist attention to the U.S. The Americans seem to have believed the Arabs liked them in that they were not the colonising British: Secretary of State Cordell Hull commented in 1942 that the U.S. was popular in the Mideast because of "a century of American missionary, educational and philanthropic efforts that have never been tarnished by any material motives or interests."[48] This perhaps gave the U.S. the feeling that she could ignore State Department and diplomatic service warnings and respond to pro-Zionist calls within the U.S. The U.S. brought about the UN partition vote, with White House staff agreeing that Truman had been determined to get a positive vote and Defence Secretary John Forrestal saying there had been "an almost scandalous use of coercion and duress upon other nations."[49] The U.S. gave Israel immediate recognition and, within the first year, a staggering $100 million loan. Britain did not give Israel *de jure* recognition until April 1950.

The second context is that of how day to day implementing of a policy was affected by events. Here Britain quickly learned that the Palestinians were not going to happily benefit from the "advantages" the Zionist scheme offered them, and had to deal with armed resistance, pressure from Arab states, pressure from the U.S. and a Zionist terrorist campaign against her. This caused constant shifts in policy. The U.S. had no practical consequences to consider and ignored pleas to share the responsibility, to offer money or men to implement the policies she was calling for; she escalated Zionist demands.

The third element is the strength of popular feeling for or against Zionism. Popular feeling was stronger in the U.S. than in

Britain, and the administration took more notice of it. Hence Truman's and Dewey's constant pro-Zionist pronouncements. This is where each country's perception of itself, its history, its myths, is important, because this explains the depth of popular Zionist feeling in the U.S. and its absence in Britain.

America, a rootless nation, clung to its sense of a mythological "past" where righteous Americans, favoured by God, exterminated the native Indians, confounded the tyrannical mother country and purified a corrupt world. There was strong identification with the Israelites, therefore with the Zionists. In Britain there was no sense of being a Chosen People nor was there a feeling of obligation to restore the Jews to Palestine.

Richard Crossman pointed out in Parliament the real gulf that separated British and American perceptions of the issue: Britain was a settled, static country, where respect for the land was strong. America was a dynamic settler country with a pioneering past. He wrote:

> The overseas settler has a different attitude from the natives like ourselves. We are like the Arabs, whereas the New Zealanders, like the Jews, have gone across the seas and they cannot take the same attitude of saying that no one can ever be allowed to go into someone else's country.... *America could have nothing but a Zionist policy in Palestine.*[50]

NOTES

1. B. Rubin, *The Arab States and the Palestinian Conflict*, p. 104.
2. *Ibid.*, p. 163.
3. *Hansard*, vol. 460, col. 935.
4. E.M. Wilson, *Decision on Palestine: How the United States Came to Recognise Israel*, Appendix 1, p. 178.
5. C.A. Rubenberg, *Israel and the American National Interest*, p. 28.
6. *Commentary*, p. 28.
7. *Ibid.*
8. A. Lilienthal, *The Zionist Connection*, p. 212.
9. *Hansard*, vol. 460, col. 952.
10. *Hansard*, vol. 460, col., 964.
11. *Hansard*, vol. 460, col. 930; Bevin quotes from the 1922 Command Paper.
12. J. Dimbleby, *The Palestinians*, p. 67.
13. *Right of Self-Determination of the Palestinian People*, p. 22; quoting Statement of Policy Cmd. 1700, 1922.
14. Cmd. 5513, 1937, p. 3.
15. F. Stark, *East is West*, pp. 61, 127.

16. P.P. Allen, *Zionist Military Preparations for Statehood*, p. 180.
17. *Hansard*, vol. 460, col. 1007.
18. *Near East Report*, November 5, 1990.
19. Sir J. Glubb, *Peace in the Holy Land—the Historical Analysis of the Palestine Problem*, p. 287.
20. D.S. Wyman, *Abandonment of the Jews*, p. 358.
21. J.H. Wilson, *The Chariot of Israel*, p. 128.
22. D.S. Wyman, *Abandonment of the Jews*, p.121.
23. *Ibid*.
24. *Hansard*, vol. 460, col. 1007.
25. J. Dimbleby, *The Palestinians*, p. 87.
26. P.P. Allen, *Zionist Military Preparations for Statehood*, p. 213.
27. *Jerusalem Post International*, 23 March 1991.
28. *Ibid*., 6 April 1991.
29. C.A. Rubenberg, *Israel and the American National Interest*, p.384, note 52.
30. *Jerusalem Post International*, 5 May 1990.
31. J. Dimbleby, *The Palestinians*, p. 84.
32. *Hansard*, vol. 460, col. 952.
33. S.L. Spiegel, *The Other Arab-Israeli Conflict: Making America's Middle East Policy, from Truman to Reagan*, p. 11.
34. *Hansard*, vol. 460, col. 1001.
35. M.E. Marty, *Pilgrims in Their Own Land*, p. 63.
36. *Ibid*.
37. *Ibid*., p. 218.
38. Commencement Address, William Woods College, Fulton, Missouri, January 1952.
39. F, Stark, *East is West*, p. 61.
40. *Hansard*, vol. 460, col. 932.
41. D. Fromkin. *A Peace to End All Peace*, p. 523.
42. *Hansard*, vol. 460, col. 955.
43. *Right of Self-Determination of the Palestinian People*, quoting Public Record Office, Foreign Office, no. 371/4183, 1919
44. Hansard, vol. 460, col. 995.
45. *Hansard*, vol. 460, col. 1015.
46. F. Stark, *East is West*, p. 105.
47. *Hansard*, vol. 460, col. 982.
48. B. Rubin, *The Great Powers in the Middle East 1941-1947: The Road to the Cold War*, p. 25.
49. J. Dimbleby, *The Palestinians*, p. 86.
50. *Hansard*, vol. 460, col. 987 (emphasis added).

AMERICAN JEWS, THE ISRAELI LOBBY, AND 1,000 DAYS OF INTIFADA

The Palestinian intifada started on December 8, 1987; by late 1990, an Israeli Army officer estimated that 625 Palestinians had been killed in clashes with the army, 14,000 Palestinians placed under administrative arrest and 70,000 Palestinians imprisoned.[1] The Palestinians themselves gave higher figures: after a thousand days of intifada, 708 Palestinians had been killed by the Israeli Army, and there had been curfews, closures of universities, dynamiting of houses, imprisonments and house arrests and other denials of civil rights.[2] This article addresses the change that these 1,000 days brought about in the attitude of American Jews and the Israeli lobby's response to this change of attitude. It will explore the monopolising of the status of victim, and the diabolising of the PLO and its then Chairman Arafat, to show how the intifada and surrounding issues were presented to an American Jewish audience, this audience wielding a certain degree of political power within the U.S., through the AIPAC. A risk was perceived: if the image of Israel, or that of the PLO or the Palestinians in the occupied territories, were sufficiently changed, this would affect the sympathies of American Jews, thus the Israeli lobby, and consequently U.S. policy itself.

The American Jewish community, which empowered the Israeli lobby in the U.S., did not constitute a monolithic bloc. Its extent and diversity have been described by Lee O'Brien in American Jewish Organisations and Israel[3]; she remarks that the *American Jewish Yearbook* mentions over two hundred national organisations, and classifies them as either Zionist, Community, Fund-raising, Political and Special Focus organisations. Where the Jewish community in America lacks a shared idea of what exactly constitutes Jewishness, since it is split into Republican and Democrat (politically), Orthodox, Reform, Conservative and non-practising (religious identity) and Zionist and anti-Zionist (pre-1948 stance), Israel has constituted a unifying focus. "The community can only be united insofar as it has areas of mutual concern to all its members; within American Jewry, there is one primary concern, namely Israel."[4] Back in 1962, I. Goldstein wrote of the one common denominator, "the feeling that we are one people with one destiny and that the Jewish State is the heart which pumps vitality into Jewish life everywhere."5

This sense of Jewish self-identification derives *inter alia* from participation in fund-raising for Israel. From the pre-1948 period, organised Zionism "set for itself the task of winning the support of the entire Jewish community" in America; by 1960, it was "enlisting financial and moral support for Israel"6 and instilling a sense of the centrality of Israel via education: "Organized Zionism in America has no more urgent task than to make a fight for intensive Hebraic, Israel-oriented Jewish education."7 Twenty years later Israel was still being promoted as a centralising force to bind the community together: pride in Israel's military record and "democratic" character (as presented by community leaders and press reports), community pro-Israel action and fund-raising (money for development, humanitarian, cultural and educational ends), settlement of oleh—thus confirming the sense of Jewishness for those who had not made aliya—merged to give a sense of community identity; "pro-Israelism has become the dominant ideological construct; the result is that various forms of Israel support work are on the agenda of virtually all Jewish establishment organizations, be they communal, welfare, religious or educational."8 The idea was still alive in 1992:

> Reform and Conservative Jews in America have an obligation to support Israel, because it continues to be the single most effective means of instilling pride in our young people and because history has shown that the Jewish people needs its own homeland.9

Specific issues which might undermine American Jewish support for Israel were minimised. Thus, issues on which American Jews might feel strongly but differently (and where in any case they were powerless to influence the Israeli government) such as the 1982 invasion of Lebanon, Israel's role in Iran-Contra, Israel's military ties with South Africa, etc., would be countered by proposing a threat to Israel that the U.S. Jews, being geographically removed from such a danger, could neither appreciate nor evaluate. When the intifada forced American Jews to question not only Israel's handling of the rising (on American television Palestinian women and children were shown as victims) but as an extension other of the Shamir Government's policies, there was a risk that dissatisfaction with the acts of a specific government could produce sympathy for the PLO or for Palestinian goals.

But when an Arab danger was proposed and the Palestinians were depicted as supporting Saddam Hussein, the original construct of an Israel in danger was given new force, and American Jews were brought back to the pro-Israel, anti-PLO fold.

Before the intifada, the American Jewish community was a well-educated, high status, well integrated community, politically effective and informed with a construct which partly depended on their receiving "correct" information about Israel, this information fed by reports, visits, media articles, communications from Jewish organisations, fund-raising drives, etc. Five and a half million in number, and representing 2.7% of the total American population (roughly the same proportion as the American Muslims, estimated the American Arab Anti-Discrimination Committee in 1991), they exercised so much influence over the administration that the Israeli lobby was referred to by some as "The Opposition" and by Rep. Mervyn M. Dymally as "without question the most effective lobby in Congress," and this Congress by Patrick Buchanan as "Israeli-occupied territory."[10]

This lobby, organised from 1951 and named AIPAC from 1959, had as its purpose "lobbying on behalf of the American Jewish community in support of Israel."[11] Its aim was also to present the views of the current Israeli Government and to influence American politicians. In 1988 with 55,000 members and a budget of $6.6 million,[12] it acted to discipline decision-makers and politicians, by literature such as the weekly *Near East Report* (some 60,000 copies circulated free of charge to Congressmen and other opinion-formers), by giving publicity, particularly in the *NER*, to politicians who supported Israel and withdrawing support from perceived enemies (an "Enemies list" was published)—"That kind of pressure is bound to affect Senators' thinking, especially if they are wavering or need support"[13]—and by organising letter-writing or telephoning campaigns.[14] AIPAC's then executive director, Thomas Dine, was quoted by O'Brien as stating: "We not only express political power, we exercise it" and was seen as "forthcoming in defense of lobbying as a proper political activity for the Jewish community."[15]

As a registered lobby, AIPAC could not give money for political ends; this was done by the back-up Political Action Committees.[16] Much has been written on their funding of pro-Israel candidates, especially for important posts, such as the Senate and House Appropriations committees, and on the influence of the organised Jewish vote, which could be decisive in areas such as New

York, New Jersey, Pennsylvania, Florida and California. Presidential candidates, mayors and party chairmen competed for the support of AIPAC; it was accepted that candidates would make rote speeches of support for Israel, thus creating a political culture where the norm was supportive.[17] Congressmen's voting patterns were checked; the November 1988 Washington *Report on Middle East Affairs* described the targeting and rewarding of candidates, mentioning the $2 million contributed by pro-Israel PACs that year to 262 candidates. Although there were only 8 Jewish Senators and 29 Jewish Representatives in the 1986 Congress, a tight group worked together to introduce resolutions and see that they were voted through; the *NER* would give credit for this in its pages. AIPAC continued to wield such power that when Clinton won the 1992 presidential elections, its president, David Steiner, made what were later called "exaggerated" claims about its influence over Clinton and its power to nominate politicians.[18] (Steiner had to resign in November 1992 when his boasts, recorded on tape, were made public)

A shared discourse, and a constant attention to providing the informational base to maintain this discourse, made AIPAC effective. A lobby out of step with the major preoccupations and perceptions of the U.S. would have had little chance of winning support, but a lobby which shared certain assumptions and knew how to present and package its discourse could be influential. While American politicians had fairly little knowledge of the Palestinian cause, they were regularly informed on Israel's views in a way which would dovetail with the U.S.'s interests and perceptions. In regional policy, Israel and the U.S. were shown as working together in the Middle East to protect Western access to oil and to bar the region to the Soviet Union (though Mark Curtis points out that in reality "secret planning documents are explicit about the absence of any real threat from the Soviet Union to Western interests in the Third World," even in the three Middle East countries—Turkey, Persia and Afghanistan— exposed to direct Soviet attack.[19]) In Central America mutual enemies were identified (the Soviets, Libya and the PLO), and Israel was valued as a conduit for U.S. arms sales to states whose human rights record precluded direct purchase from the U.S. The two countries' spy systems were tied together, with Mossad and the CIA working in harmony and strong personal contacts being formed. There was also a shared sense of religious destiny, especially felt by American fundamentalist Christians, and a perceived shared cultural identity.

The Palestinians had no similar lobby. The American Arab Anti-Discrimination Committee was more of a "defence" organisation (like B'nai B'rith) than a lobby; the older National Association of Arab Americans was ill-funded, weak and timid. It was also splintered; as its former president J.D. Baroody remarked: "The Israeli Government has one policy to state, whereas we couldn't represent 'the Arabs' if we wanted to. They're as different as the Libyans and Saudis are different, or as divided as the Christian and Moslem Lebanese."[20] The Palestinians were a small minority of American Arabs, numbering only 150,000 out of a total almost 3 million. Nor did the Palestinians share a discourse with Americans; neither cultural, historical or religious constructs existed to bind them together: Arab cultural and emotional values were unlike the American values of individualism, immediacy and self-expression; the pioneering ethic was closer to Israeli expansionism than to the Palestinian desire to retain land, and Judaism was seen as the forerunner to Christianity, whereas Islam was the aggressive rival—both as a religion and as a civilisation. The media reinforced these perceptions; Jewish writers contributing to the major and syndicated papers knew how to manipulate the idiom, tone and reference of American prose, while the few Palestinian writers—with the exception of Edward Said—had far less effect.

The Israeli lobby was powerful in that it presented itself as representing a solid bloc of Jewish opinion. If this opinion became less monolithic, if AIPAC's representativeness were questioned, or if AIPAC itself were to question Israel's policies, the U.S. administration would be able to act with freer hands. Did the intifada change either the American Jews' views, or their agreement that AIPAC represented these, or AIPAC itself?

A change did take place in American Jews' views on Israel. For the first time, leaders began to ask whether Israel was the ideal democracy they had imagined, whether peace with the Arab states was possible, whether the PLO could be a negotiating partner, and whether and in what way the occupied territories could be returned. This was accompanied by a more critical attitude to Israel's handling of relations with the U.S.—the "Who's a Jew?" problem, whereby the status of the (mostly non-Orthodox) American Jews was questioned,[21] the Jonathan Pollard spy scandal and the Shin Bet cover-up of the July 28, 1989 kidnapping of Sheikh Obeid.

Criticism of Israel, particularly voiced among young American Jews, focused first on her handling of the intifada and then by extension on her relations with the U.S. and the Israeli system itself. The February 1989 State Department report on Israel's human rights violations, and the subsequent reporting by Sen. P.J. Leahy and Rep. R.R. Obey on how such behaviour was perceived by Americans, affected the Jewish community; the new Law of Return, which discriminated against non-Orthodox Jews, caused uneasy speculation that the Jewish community was seen as second class and only valued for its financial help; the wheeling and dealing mode in which the Israeli Government tried to pick up Orthodox support presented Israel as one country among others, not unique. Support for Israel came to be seen as distinct from support for the current Israeli Government. Prime Minister Shamir's visits to the U.S. intensified this feeling, partly because Shamir did not try to placate the American Jews and obviously refused to believe them when they told him their views.

Dissatisfaction with the Shamir Government's handling of the intifada was expressed by a dissenting Jewish organisation, the American Council for Judaism (ACJ). This group, traditionally known for its critical stance, found it easier than other, more pro-Israel, groups to voice the feelings of critical American Jews; it still covered its back, however, by using Israeli writers and statesmen (Abba Eban, Abi Rath, David Grossman, Meron Benvenisti, Amos Oz) as references. For the ACJ, the "intifada's message has reached the minds of America's young as little else has done.... Is Israel as bad as she seems to be now? Is there no peace to be found?" It quoted an anonymous Columbia University senior: "I thought Israel was a place where hard-working Jews were righteously trying to hold onto a tiny piece of land. Then I find out that what they've been doing all these years is highly immoral to the people living there.... The issue is so explosive because people feel they've been fooled." The ACJ presented the intifada as weakening "forty years of loyalty" and attracting criticism "of the shambles the government has made of putting down the upheaval and also of every facet of Israel's military, economic, religious, political and social life."[22]

The American Jewish Committee (AJC), whose role was to liaise with politicians and business, church and labour leaders on Israel's behalf, gradually exchanged its 1983 certainty that pro-Israel feeling was pervasive among U.S. Jews for a recognition that American Jews were finding fault with Israel's handling of the intifada. In its fairly extensive literature on the intifada, it first (December 23, 1987) portrayed the rising as "pure PLO incitement," a "bloody scenario [that was] conceived and orchestrated by PLO's Fatah and Islamic fundamentalists" to show that the PLO was still alive, and blamed Palestinians who incited violence. By February 26, 1988, while stating that "American Jews' commitment to Israel has in no way been weakened by their anguish over the current violence there," it admitted that reports of Israeli violence could be reducing sympathy with Israel. In an open letter to the people of Israel, published in the 2 February 1988 *Jerusalem Post*, AJC President Theodore Ellenoff, while stressing the unity of the U.S. Jewish communities and Israel, warned: "Because we identify so closely with you, it has been hard for many American Jews to accept" Israel's actions: "We do not expect you to be nice in order to satisfy some of our illusions about Israel, but we do expect a certain level of decency from a country whose fortunes are so intertwined with ours." Although the AJC would "continue to interpret your agony and dilemma to our community," this would now depend on the way in which Israel handled the uprising. In an admission that some people felt sympathy for the intifada victims, the AJC argued that the stone-throwers were "perhaps civilians but they're also fighters."[23] But it did express anxiety about the treatment these stone-throwers might meet with after Rabin's "might and beatings" speech, while accepting Shamir's promise that excessive force would not be used. Thus the AJC, a major Jewish group, came to express a degree of anxiety and criticism that was unusual.

There were expressions of dismay that Israel could betray a perceived tradition of Jewish humanitarianism. Jewish writers such as Woody Allen, Arthur Miller, Betty Friedan and Philip Roth took out an advertisement in *The New York Times* in April, 1989, to denounce Shamir's policies as "immoral, contrary to what is best in our Jewish tradition and destructive to the best interests of Israel and American Jewry."[24] Figureheads such as former Conference of Presidents of Major American Jewish Organizations head Joseph Setin, Hadassah's Ruth Popkin, the AJC's Gold and Rabbi Alexander Schindler declared that Israel's repressive treatment of Palestinians violated every principle of decency.

This was accompanied by a feeling of frustration that Shamir seemed deaf to their anxiety. When at a June 1989 meeting with Senators he dismissed a list of Palestinian children killed, there was a hostile reaction. The critical magazine *Tikkun* proposed that the

Shamir Government's handling of the intifada had precipitated the greatest crisis facing American Jewry since the Holocaust. In their discomfort, some U.S. Jews started to display a tendency "to withdrawal, to ignoring what is happening.... So they will talk about 'Who is a Jew,' or aid to Soviet emigrants. They don't want to hear about the intifada."[25]

Criticism of Israeli violence led to a questioning of other assumptions. The demonising of an enemy is an important element in any struggle; any change in the mythic perceived status of Arafat, the PLO or the Palestinians would materially affect the positions of the combatants in the Israeli/Palestinian struggle. During the intifada, a change did take place in the manner in which American Jews viewed the Palestinians. The myth of the PLO, larger than life and infinitely destructive, promoted not only by Israel and AIPAC but also by writers such as G.F. Will, N. Podhoretz, W. Safire and A.M. Rosenthal gave way to a more realistic assessment of the PLO's members, aims and capabilities. Abba Eban ridiculed the myth of a tiny Israel confronting a powerful enemy:

> the PLO forces, by contrast, are depicted as the lineal descendants of Alexander the Great, Genghis Khan, Napoleon and the Hitler and Stalin dictatorships, able to exterminate Israel...The Israeli defense system is one of the wonders of the world, whereas the PLO had 8,000 men in scattered places, zero tanks and aircraft, a few guns and no missiles.[26]

Ezer Weizman echoed this appreciation of the relative strengths of Israel and the PLO. Before the Knesset abolished the Law Against Contacts with the PLO (January 1993) Weizman met illegally with PLO members (for this he was dismissed from his post and placed under surveillance); when reminded that the PLO wanted to destroy Israel, his thought was that "we have one of the best air forces in the world and a good little army so when people say that the PLO wants to destroy us, I piddle myself with laughter."[27]

As events changed perceptions, and as Israeli writers like Eban challenged the American writers' assumptions, the construct of a beleaguered Israel, surrounded by millions of Arabs devoted to its elimination, eternal victim and righteous, was confronted with another construct: Palestinian victims in an occupied land, existing in their own right as a people with rights and their own distinct perspective on the Arab/Israeli conflict. It was not that American Jews embraced this construct; rather, for the first time, they admitted that it could exist. Arafat was cut down from monstrous size, stripped of his demonic dimension, to become a leader whose pronouncements need not be automatically disbelieved. The Arab/Muslim (with all its connotations), Soviet-supported (ditto) Palestinian became a human being (a child, a bereaved woman, a family whose house had been dynamited, a Christian). The perceptual framework within which they placed the Israeli/Palestinian conflict changed. Where before the intifada the Palestinians had been seen only as the "Other," perceived in terms of the Israelis' self-image, and by extension the American Jews' self-image, they now acquired an identity of their own. (It should be remembered that place names, for example, were always given as the Israeli names, not the Arab, and that acts of violence perpetrated by Israelis were seen as acts of unbalanced individuals where Palestinian acts of violence were seen as "terrorist" vindictively planned and perpetrated.) But the intifada gave the Palestinians human and individual status in their own right. The American Jewish attitude to the various dimensions of the problem (status of Arafat and the PLO, existence of Palestinians as a distinct people, possibility of these Palestinians choosing their representatives to take part in a peace process where land would be exchanged for peace, role of the U.S. and position of AIPAC in influencing the U.S. administration) underwent a fundamental shift during the first 1,000 days of intifada.

The Israeli view of the PLO and its Chairman had been apocalyptic. Prime Minister Begin had seen Arafat and the PLO in terms of Hitler and the Nazis: "Never in the history of mankind has there been an armed organization so loathsome and contemptible, with the exception of the Nazis," he declared, and he compared the destruction of Arafat's headquarters in Beirut with an Israeli Army going into Berlin to destroy Hitler in his bunker.[28] This comparison was defended by Herzl Rosenblum, editor of *Yediot Aharonot*:

> Arafat, were he only to get enough power, would do to us things that even Hitler never imagined. This is not rhetoric on our part. If Hitler killed us with a certain restraint—were Arafat ever to come to power, he would not merely play at such matters. He would cut off our children's heads with a war shriek, rape our women in broad daylight before tearing them to shreds.... Begin, when he began speaking recently about Hitler, did not exaggerate—in fact, he minimized—the danger lying in wait for us from the mad rise of this mass murderer from Beirut.[29]

Although this was not a universally held view in Israel, it was important in informing the American Jews' vision of the PLO and its Chairman.

A change, however, took place. It is visible in the literature of the American Jewish Committee: on December 23, 1987 the AJC still referred to Arafat in terms of his "Force 17" and as "inciting Palestinians," "trying to buy life at the expense of the lives of Palestinians and Israelis" in a "murderous course." By March 10, 1988 its president, Theodore Ellenoff, was still depicting the PLO as "an intransigent band of cold-blooded murderers for whom the political process is empty rhetoric" and warning against any idea that Arafat "genuinely seeks accommodation and compromise," but the fact that he felt the need to issue the warning in itself shows that a certain shift had taken place. By March 16, an analysis by G.E. Gruen for the AJC admitted that as "leaders of the Palestinian unrest inside the territories, whatever their internal differences, acknowledge the PLO's primacy in formulating overall policy" it was necessary to examine the PLO's position. Stating, however, that the PLO made dissimilar pronouncements to Arab and American audiences, it warned that it "has not moderated its fundamental stand. Not only does it seek to undermine the peace process, but it still intends to erase the state of Israel from the map"; the PLO's "continuing resort to terrorist actions pose [sic] a serious threat not merely to individual Israelis but to American efforts to achieve a comprehensive and lasting peace." But by October 31, 1988 (by which time Arafat had given his 14 September speech to the European Parliament), Arafat had become "Chairman Arafat," presented as more moderate than those who were now denouncing him for capitulation and treason. The next step was a reaction to the PLO's November 15 proclamation of the state of Palestine and its proposal that peace talks should be started on the basis of a two-state solution. Here the AJC's 18 November report warned that the PLO still viewed Israel as a racist state, was probably still operating the "strategy of stages" and still intended the elimination of Israel, but Arafat had now become "Mr. Arafat" (repeatedly) and it was allowed that his "empty rhetoric" could betray a search for peace. By December 8, an AJC report admitted that Arafat had met with five prominent American Jews (one of them, Rita Hauser, a vice president of the AJC though not present in that capacity), and hopes were expressed that when he addressed the UN General Assembly he would "help allay Israeli fears and clear up the remaining ambiguities in the PLO's position." The fact that the AJC printed Rita Hauser's call for the U.S. administration to start direct talks with the PLO, saying she was certain American Jews would approve, showed the distance the AJC had travelled since the previous year.[30]

As attitudes to Arafat and the PLO changed, some felt the Palestinians themselves should be consulted in decisions on the region's future. The "Jordanian option" was increasingly supplanted by the idea of finding first a group of non-PLO Palestinians, then "moderate Palestinian leaders who renounce violence and formally recognise Israel," "local Arab leadership,"[31] and finally a mixed group of resident Palestinians and PLO members to take part in the peace talks. In surveys, an increasing number of U.S. Jews approved the idea of talks between Israel and the PLO. In 1979, 20% approved; by January 1989, 30% approved; in an April 1989 survey 58% approved; and in an October-November 1989 poll 73% approved of talks with the PLO on condition it recognise Israel and renounce terrorism, while 46% approved with no conditions attached.[32]

There was also a change of approach on the issue of settlements, where a certain ambiguity already existed. From President Carter on, the U.S. administration had opposed settlement activity (thus a question of dual loyalty could arise); extreme right-wing Jews saw settlements as the working out of a divine plan whereas others considered them provocative; some, while condemning them in principle saw them as necessary to help incoming Soviet Jews; others viewed settlements in the West Bank as unlike settlements in East Jerusalem, or where Arab property in Israeli Jerusalem was concerned.

Where there were many views, there was little information as to the amount of land taken for settlement activity, the diversion from Arab villages of water and electricity, etc., or the Government's tax policy of encouragement for settlers. And since, unlike the intifada, settlement activity did not make for gripping television, American Jews were comparatively uninformed on this less evidently emotional issue. Though the AJC in 1988 stuck by its 1978 statement that settlements were not inherently illegal, and its 1980 statement that "Jews have a right to live in the West Bank," it made the condition that "settlement activity should not be such as to impede the peace process."[33] Some confusion still remained; the Israel-Diaspora Institute found in a poll held in October/November 1989 that many U.S. Jews would not oppose a statement viewing settlements as illegal, and 314 of those polled spoke out against settlements and against annexing the occupied territories.

Linked to the settlements issue was that of the eventual possibility of land-for-peace. While from 1967 the U.S. had seen these territories as distinct from Israel, to be used as bargaining counters in a peace process, the Shamir Government's stance was clearly different: Israel had given land to Egypt and thus fully implemented Resolution 242. (Shamir's declared intention was to promote settlements to such an extent that the occupied territories would never revert to Palestinian control.)

Tentatively, the American Jewish community began to change its position. The AJC first said the concerned parties—Israel and a Jordanian/Palestinian delegation—must decide about "power-sharing provisions" in the territories.[34] Then, after Arafat's declaration of a Palestinian state, it expressed anxiety about a Palestinian stage-by-stage strategy, citing statements made by Ahmed Abdel-Rahman, Sheikh Abdel-Hamid el-Sayah and Abu Iyad. It felt that this eventuality, whereby Israel could be whittled away, would be prevented if the PLO supported repeal of the UN resolution (3379) and recognised the legitimacy of Israel.[35] A sense of at least the possibility of land for peace was promoted when it circulated a *Reuters* report citing Arafat: "The PLO accepted two states, a Palestinian state and a Jewish state, Israel. Is that clear enough?" and Prof. Abraham Udovitch, a member of the Jewish delegation meeting Arafat: "A deep and historic change has taken place...on the question of the existence of and co-existence with Israel."[36] The American Council for Judaism, already mentioned as more traditionally critical of Israel, was more positive, showing how Jews in London and Israel and the U.S. were urging Israel to end her occupation and allow Palestinian statehood, and citing a former CPMAJO chairman as welcoming Bassam Abu Sharif's call for direct peace talks between Israel and the PLO.[37]

By December 1988, U.S. Jews were expressing a variety of stances ranging from Morris B. Abram's suspicions (he was chairman of the CPMAJO) that Arafat's acceptance of Israel was "meaningless" unless the PLO renounced its Charter and the Arab League its refusal to recognise Israel as legitimate, to less suspicious views. Rabbi Alexander M. Schindler, president of the Union of American Hebrew Congregations, and Rabbi Arthur Hertzberg, former vice-president of the World Jewish Congress, held hopeful views. By this time, five U.S. Jews had actually met with Arafat.

This met with vitriolic condemnation and reference to the Holocaust (Milton Shapiro of the Zionist Organization of America), mild criticism as being misplaced (Rabbi Jerome M. Epstein of the United Synagogue of America), or support from "prominent American Jews."[38] A new group, set up by *Tikkun*, the Committee for Judaism and Social Justice, called for talks with the PLO that could result in the setting up of a Palestinian state. By October 1989, B'nai B'rith said it would not oppose a Palestinian homeland.[39]

Once the idea had been mooted, increasing support emerged for land-for-peace and a Palestinian state. Fewer U.S. Jews disapproved of the possibility of the latter than before.[40] A poll published in November 1989, funded by the AJC, showed that a 2㌼1 majority of U.S. Jews favoured a Palestinian homeland as long as it did not threaten Israel's security.[41] By February 1990, three-fourths of Jews polled called for territorial compromise in the West Bank and Gaza, and 67-81% approved of a Palestinian "state" or "homeland" or "sovereignty," depending on the term used, while 59% favoured a demilitarized Palestinian state, after 15 years of confidence-building.[42] In May, *Time* reported that "evidence abounds that all but a few of the 38 Jewish members of Congress" favoured land-for peace, though they did not wish to say so publicly.[43]

After decades of reticence, American Jews set up new groups to promote land-for-peace. "Americans for Peace Now" was one, "Americans for Peace in the Middle East," made up of academics and politicians, another. Its head, Dr. Alon Ben-Meir, said that Israel, whether or not she had a historical right to the occupied territories, would have to be content with less. "Both sides must be satisfied, Israel with part of the promised land, and the Palestinians with a piece of Palestine." Neither state would be ethnically pure—"There will always be a Palestinian minority in Israel, and vice-versa."[44]

Another issue where positions changed was that of U.S./Palestinian talks. When these finally started, the expected fury from the Jewish community did not materialise, much to the surprise of State Department officials and indeed of many Jewish groups.

The PLO and the USSR had long insisted on the need to implement UN resolutions and to hold an international conference to resolve the Palestinian question. The U.S. had felt this would subject Israel to one-sided pressure from the Soviet Union, China and the Europeans. The PLO realised that as long as the U.S. supported Israel and was less well informed on the Palestinian case, there would be no possibility of an international conference being held, and therefore proposed a dialogue with the U.S. Obviously, as the image of the PLO improved, the probability of the U.S. administration talking to it increased. But there was widespread uneasiness about the reaction of the American Jews.

The AJC first expressed its fear that an international conference "which would bestow a continuing substantive role upon the permanent members of the UN Security Council (including the USSR and China), would serve to pressure, isolate and pillory Israel"[45]; it opposed a conference with any role other than ceremonial ("Moscow insists that the five permanent members of the Security Council have a continuing and substantive role") or where "the PLO designate the Palestinian delegation."[46] It felt that any effective international conference held on the basis of UN resolutions 242 and 338 might lead to a smaller Israel. It then noted that the PLO was trying "to convince the new administration of President-elect George Bush to begin a dialogue with the PLO"[47] and warned readers that the PLO had not met U.S. conditions for discussions. By December 1988, when the U.S. started its dialogue with the PLO, the AJC accepted that the talks had begun but urged the administration (stressing America's long-standing support for Israel) to use the agreement to talk to demand still further concessions from Arafat. But it admitted that the hostile reaction expected from U.S. Jews had not materialised; there had not been one single angry phone call. "People accept the American Government's decision, even knowing that it is opposed in Tel Aviv. This is an entirely new situation. We are now in uncharted waters," said David Harris of the AJC.[48] Indeed, former CPMAJO president Seymour Reich stated that almost all American Jews were in favour of the talks. This was an exaggeration, disproved by the January 1989 poll, where only 30% of U.S. Jews supported the dialogue; however, this was greater than previously.[49] In a November poll the majority of U.S. Jews was found to support the talks. The Israeli ambassador, Netanyahu, was displeased at what he called a weak and ineffective response.

Not all American Jewish leaders approved. Morris Abram decided that he could trust Shultz, since Shultz was known to be against a Palestinian state so Israel was in safe hands; Rabbi Abbi Veiss (Coalition of Concern) charged that the U.S. was "capitulating to murderers and thugs" and the Zionists of America that the administration was "naive" and the PLO "terrorists."[50]

Lastly, the intifada changed the American Jews" attitude to AIPAC. Formerly perceived as representing a monolithic bloc of opinion—and thus constituting (according to the State Department) a powerful constraint on U.S. policy—it came to be viewed by some U.S. Jews as misrepresenting their feelings. In October 1988 the AJC, the American Jewish Congress and B'nai B'rith decided to set up an alternative lobby. A Jewish Committee on the Middle East was founded. Michael Lerner's magazine *Tikkun* (an alternative to the traditional *Commentary,* and described 13 July 1991 by the *Jerusalem Post International* as providing a "steady stream of anti-Israel bias and poison") set up in 1989 the Committee for Judaism and Social Justice to act as a liberal alternative to AIPAC and the CPMAJO.[51] In the same year the Jewish Peace Lobby promoted the idea of preserving Israel's security while accepting the Palestinians' right to self-determination and perhaps to a demilitarized Palestinian state.[52] A branch of Peace Now, Americans for Peace Now, formed in 1990 to present an alternative to AIPAC. As regards funding, in 1989 a New Israel Fund was set up to promote civil rights, religious pluralism and Jewish-Arab coexistence, aims which David Arnow, on its directing board, said would have previously been seen as anti-Israel.[53]

"AIPAC is the object of surprising dissent within the Jewish community," reported *Time*, May 7, 1990, citing the discordance between what polls showed American Jews as feeling and what AIPAC presented as their attitude. It pointed out that as Israeli opinion was split over the Palestine issue, so would American Jewry also be split, and that "in synagogues and Jewish community centers across the U.S., speakers who a few years ago were labelled 'self-hating Jews' and worse for advocating compromise with the Palestinians are routinely welcomed and applauded, though often uneasily."

AIPAC's approach was felt by many Jews to reflect too closely the position of the Shamir Government. When in March 1990 Thomas Dine criticised President Bush for damaging the peace process by stating that East Jerusalem was occupied territory ("Suddenly there is a rejoicing at PLO headquarters and dismay in Israel"[54]), Rita Hauser replied that on the contrary it was Shamir who was stalling on the peace process, and that AIPAC's anti-Bush stance was outrageous. Similarly, the Union of American Hebrew Congregations and the American Jewish Congress felt that their views were not being correctly represented by AIPAC. A statement printed in *The Nation, The New York Review of Books* and other papers called for a re-evaluation of America's sponsorship of Israel and asked for cuts in aid, reduced military and intelligence help and a U.S. dissociation from Israeli politics—all anathema to AIPAC.

The Israeli lobby's strength had been such that, unlike the Arab lobby, it had been seen as representing the democratically-expressed wishes of all American Jews. When an alternative lobby was proposed, or when American Jews expressed views that conflicted with those of AIPAC, the U.S. administration (thus ran the argument) would feel freer to act. American Jews explained their new attitude as still supportive of Israel, but in a more realistic manner. "Here in the U.S. we are trying to persuade American Jews not to support Israel blindly, right or wrong. That doesn't serve Israel's interests," said Dr. Alon Ben-Meir, leader of Americans for Peace in the Middle East.[55]

AIPAC did, however, retain its other power: the ability to influence politicians by targeting campaign money against those who stepped out of line. Even in May 1990, an aide to a Jewish Congressman was quoted as saying that politicians were still voting for Israeli stances: "Sometimes the only explanation is that for politicians the cost of opposing Israel is still greater than the cost of not supporting it."[56] He wondered whether it was possible that at some point Israel might push Congress or the U.S. Jews too far. AIPAC, at this point in time, believed that it still had control over American politics as far as funding was concerned: the U.S. was still giving Israel the usual $1.8 billion in military aid and $1.2 billion in economic aid, plus an extra $400 million in loan guarantees (agreed by Congress in February, and by the Administration in September, 1990).

But the shift in the attitude of some American Jews still caused anxiety; a reaction from the AIPAC and some of the more Zionist of the American Jewish organisations followed. The new tactics included visits from Yitzhak Shamir, a condemning of the "court Jews" who deviated from the Israeli line, and insistence that only the Shamir Government could appreciate the particular danger that Israel was in (so American Jews should neither criticise nor make public suggestions), increased attention to the media and the discovery of an enemy—Saddam Hussein—whose actions would unite U.S. Jewry in support of Israel and against the Palestinians.

Prime Minister Shamir's visits to the U.S. were not markedly successful in uniting American Jews behind him. His perceived intransigence, at a time when American Jews were increasingly uneasy about Israel's handling of the intifada, alienated many former supporters. In March 1989 he suggested that the intifada was a revolt against Israel's existence, not against the occupation. Professing amazement at a letter from 30 Senators calling for Israel to exchange land for peace, he argued that Israel had already given up land. His proposal for Palestinian elections (once the intifada had stopped, and without the participation of the East Jerusalem Palestinians) was presented as a positive step: CPMAJO head Seymour Reich believed that the attention of American Jews could "now be directed towards this election process and not towards 'land for peace'."[57] When 3,200 Jews cheered Shamir in the New York B'nai Abraham Temple this seemed to show that he had convinced American Jews of the rightness of his position. So did the Jewish National Fund of America's pledging a $2.1 million gift, and its president Rabbi Joseph Sternstein's call for a stronger statement opposing talks with the PLO or the 2-state solution and his warning that criticism of Shamir would play into the hands of elements in the administration which were hostile to Israel.[58]

But during Shamir's November visit, 213 leading Reform and Conservative rabbis told him they believed Israel should exchange land for peace; their November 15 letter begged: "For the good of Israel and in the spirit of Jewish tradition, turn to the Palestinians, acknowledge them as equal bearers of rights, and offer to withdraw from the territories in exchange for peace and security."[59] Other prominent Jews signed a letter printed in *Tikkun* urging talks with the PLO and supporting Palestinian self-determination. (Seymour Reich depicted the signatories as a mere handful of people out of touch with mainstream Jewish feeling.) Forty-one leaders warned Shamir not to mistake politeness for support, and he was given a cool reception when addressing an audience of 3,000 in Cincinnati (at a General Assembly of the Council of Jewish Federations) and a hostile one from an audience of 900 in San Francisco (at a conference sponsored by *Tikkun*). Michael Lerner claimed that "Shamir's goal is to prevent any process involving the exchange of land for peace, while simultaneously presenting himself as trying to advance negotiations."[60] Thus, Shamir had failed to unite American Jews behind him.

A second strategy was to claim that opponents of Israel's policies were ill-informed, tactless or corrupt. Here the case of Henry Siegman is instructive. Executive director of the American Jewish Congress, with a "long and constructive history of Zionist and pro-Israel advocacy in the U.S.," he had opposed Arafat's visit to the

U.S. and then active in promoting the breaking off of U.S. talks with the PLO. But he felt Israel did not realise how badly her image was being eroded in the U.S., and wished to warn the Israeli Government about the effect caused by its "provincial, ideologically rigid and exclusivist" reading of the situation. He defended himself for having given this warning in an Israeli paper: "I said that, contrary to the soothing assurances brought here regularly by American Jewish leaders to the effect that...the fundamental ties between the U.S. and Israel remain unimpaired, it is in fact those ties that are beginning to erode." Quoting a *New York Times* poll that demonstrated this erosion, he insisted that anyone who believed "these poll results have no impact on the U.S. administration and on the U.S. Congress lives in a fool's paradise."[61] Siegman was denounced as a self-hater and belittled as the leader of a "tiny organization of a few thousand, most of whose membership is acquired through group tours,"[62] which was part of the "trendy bash-Israel crowd" and which "displays chutzpah in inverse relation to its importance"; it was implied that he had bought his presidency; it was stated that he did not really represent AJC views and that in any case the AJC's "constant public criticism of Israel" had forced Israel to put her own security at risk; that he should therefore be "assiduously shunned by all proud Jews."[63] He was reminded that those who did not live in Israel should not criticise its government, except very privately to that government[64]: "only those whose lives are on the line have the moral right" to interfere in policy decisions.[65] The AJC was accused of acting as apologist for the U.S. Administration, of being "court Jews of the worst kind"; it was suggested that Israel should ignore such bodies and instead use AIPAC or "appeal to the Jews of America directly, and favor among Jewish leaders and executives those who do not publicly hector it on what it should or should not do."[66]

The logical consequence of such advice was that any American Jewish leader who criticised Israel would be seen as a traitor; only silence in America and the Israeli media, and private words to the Israeli Government, were legitimate.

Greater attention was devoted to the media. It was proposed that the press was manipulating American Jews, sensitivity to Israel's human rights violations:

> Media manipulation of American Jews is going through a deadly cycle. First, the nature of the conflict is misrepresented. Then the media reports that American Jews are unhappy about Israel

because of what they see on TV and read in the papers. Reading such reports, American Jews who have been made unhappy feel justified when they hear that their leaders are unhappy too. Then instead of the so-called Jewish lobby being able to exert pressure on American policy to help Israel, it will be turned around to become an instrument of American pressure on Israel.[67]

It was proposed that the media was Arab dominated. In March 1990, FLAME (Facts and Logic about the Middle East) was set up under Gerardo Joffe to counter this "incessant anti-Israel and anti-Semitic propaganda by the Arabs and the native bigots."[68] FLAME described itself in its advertisements as "exposing false propaganda that might harm the interests of the United States and its allies" in the Middle East, and asked for (tax-deductible) contributions to place messages in national newspapers and magazines. The Israeli *Jerusalem Post*, whose international edition sold widely in the U.S., had printed information on Israel's nuclear industry and the Mordechai Vanunu affair, peace and left-wing groups in Israel, labour disputes in Israel and events in the occupied territories; its criticism of the Shamir Government's policies had allowed American Jews to voice anti-Shamir sentiments without feeling disloyal. Now, in 1989, it was bought by Conrad Black's Hollingermedia chain for Ariel Sharon and its editor and many columnists replaced. Its stance changed radically and much was printed on the duty of diaspora Jews to support Israel. The remaining staff complained about its new right-wing bias. Meron Benvenisti, for example, saw the paper's decision not to publish a report on human rights violations in the occupied territories (funded by the Ford and Rockefeller Foundations) as an instance of the paper's change of stance.[69]

But what really rallied American Jews to Israel in her hour of need—and dealt a blow to any sympathy with Arafat—was Iraq's invasion of Kuwait. To what extent Israel herself proposed this threat, and to what extent she was the beneficiary, is still unclear. But the result was to unite American Jews in concern for Israel's safety.

Iraq had been identified by Israel as the most dangerous of her Arab enemies. This explains the 1981 bombing of Iraq's Ozirak nuclear facility, justified by Prime Minister Begin with reference to the Holocaust: "We must protect our nation, a million and a half of whose children were murdered by the Nazis in the gas chambers."[70] A speech by the Iraqi president had been widely misquoted, stripping it of its conditional tone: Saddam Hussein had said that "if Israel commits aggression and attacks, we will strike back with great force. If Israel uses weapons of total destruction against our nation we will use whatever weapons of total destruction we have against it." This was described as the rhetoric of a madman.[71] Throughout the spring of 1990, the Israeli press carried constant references to the Iraqi danger; and U.S. Jews and politicians were reported as rallying "around Israel in the face of Iraqi President Saddam Hussein's outrageous threats."[72] Various politicians were later to recall that Israel had been vocal in pressing for war against Iraq. One of these was Patrick Buchanan, who had served in the Nixon and Reagan teams and who questioned whether the U.S.'s interests would be served by making war on Iraq to serve Israel's purposes. "There are two groups that are beating the drums...for war in the Middle East—the Israeli Defense Ministry and its amen corner in the United States.... The Israelis want this war for us to destroy the Iraqi war machine."[73] (This argument finds some support in a statement by Israel's Defence Minister, Moshe Arens to the effect that "if Saddam Hussein remains in office, and retains the weaponry he possesses, there are grounds for concern in Israel," and in the fact that during a July 1990 visit to the U.S. Arens issued a warning about Iraq's nuclear intentions.[74]) Buchanan charged that five pro-Israel journalists were pushing for a war against Iraq. He was correct in this accusation insofar as writers such as A.M. Rosenthal and William Safire were indeed calling for war. Rosenthal spoke of "appeasement" (with all its connotations), compared Saddam to Hitler and criticised U.S. politicians who had "licked Saddam Hussein's boots" while asking whether President Bush would "wait until Saddam Hussein develops nuclear bombs and ask the Israelis to go get him again"; Safire ridiculed the suggestion of imposing sanctions on Iraq and proposed war as the sole option: "We are dealing here with our own survival. As soon as Iraq gets the bomb and the missile, millions of American lives are in peril."[75]

To counter Buchanan's charges, he was accused of anti-Semitism—"spewing venom against Jews and Israel on a regular basis" and "writers such as Rosenthal and Safire, or Charles Krauthammer" and Alan Dershowitz were presented as being better equipped than Buchanan to write on Middle East issues, being "fair-minded." (Surprisingly, since Rosenthal had shared the $100,000 Defender of Jerusalem award, given to those whose actions help defend the rights of the Jewish people, and also since Rosenthal and

Safire had already been ridiculed by Israeli Abba Eban for their unrealistic views.[76]) AIPAC called on the public to contact 180 local papers syndicating Buchanan's articles to stop him being printed, and proposed a nation-wide hunt to identify other "Buchanans" and have them silenced.

The political crisis developed quickly. On 2 August 1990, Iraq invaded Kuwait; by 7 August there was a massive build-up of American troops; on 9 August the Cairo summit was called and 10 August found Arafat and four Arab delegations searching for a negotiated solution, only to learn that a final communiqué (to send a pan-Arab force to defend Saudi Arabia) had already been written and translated into English. Arafat's plan was abandoned and a vote forced on this prepared communiqué. On 11 August, the PLO and four other delegations condemned this, though simultaneously condemning Iraq's annexing of Kuwait. On 26 August, the PLO called for a UN or Arab League force in Saudi Arabia and Kuwait.

The Palestinians had not reacted as the American Jews would have wished. In the face of continuing immigration of Soviet Jews, and the existence of a right-wing government that was continuing the repression, Palestinians came out in support of Iraq—if an armed conflict were to oppose Iraq to the U.S. and Israel. Prominent Palestinians issued a statement calling for an Iraqi withdrawal, but placing this within an international context: they spoke of the inadmissibility everywhere—of acquiring land by force and the indivisibility of UN legislation, and they rejected any foreign intervention, in particular the proposed U.S. military deployment.[77] Their comparing Iraq's actions with Israel's, and their suggestion that both countries should be similarly treated, was not confined to Palestinians. The sentiments were echoed by the former Arab League ambassador to Paris, Hamadi Essid. He pointed out that the passionate support for Saddam found among Palestinians and Third World populations sprang from their feeling that Saddam had confronted Israel's protector—the U.S.—which had allowed Israel to ignore all the negotiated solutions to the Israeli/Palestinian problem that had been suggested by the PLO, the Arab League or the UN; he also insisted that the argument that Israel should have the nuclear weapon but not Iraq was one that could not be accepted by Arabs.[78]

Faisal Husseini insisted that the PLO had never supported Iraq's occupation of Kuwait. The PLO Executive Committee statement of 19 August 1990 repeated this, adding that the PLO had tried to solve the crisis by dialogue, as it had in the 1972 Kuwait/Iraqi crisis; it had met with other Arab leaders and persuaded Saddam Hussein to attend an Arab summit; it was certain that Iraq intended to discuss arrangements with Kuwait and also Iraqi and Israeli withdrawals; it was at that moment relaying further proposals to the UN Security Council and the UN Secretary General, the non-aligned group and the Arab countries. It repeatedly stated that it opposed Iraq's invasion but hoped for a negotiated settlement, and insisted that Israel's continued occupation of Palestinian land should also be addressed.[79] This point was clearly made at the 7th UN International NGO Meeting on the Question of Palestine, where concern was expressed at Israel's continuing repression of Palestinians, destruction of Palestinian culture and settling of Jews in the territories, and the U.S.'s suspension of dialogue with the PLO, and which called on both Iraq and Israel to withdraw from the territories they had occupied.[80]

In November, Abu Iyad again presented the PLO's position: "It had been against the invasion of Kuwait but had not wanted to condemn Iraq and thus justify the American presence in Saudi Arabia." A link had to be made between the Kuwaiti and Palestinian questions: "Let's try to apply the same logic everywhere. If we pressure Iraq, why not Israel?"[81]

But the PLO's attempts to present an even-handed approach and to negotiate a peaceful settlement were rarely reported in the Western media. An exception was the writer Paul Lalor, who recognised that the PLO had condemned Iraq's action and was committed to the Arab League Charter, which precludes Arab intervention in the affairs of another Arab state. The crisis, moreover,

> distracted world attention from the Israeli-Palestine conflict, providing Israel with the perfect opportunity to suppress the uprising and settle new immigrants in the occupied territories. Hard won international sympathy for the Palestinian cause, particularly among Israelis and American Jews, would swing against them once again and the concept of "fortress Israel" the reliable ally in a volatile region, would gain greater support.[82]

The PLO gained no credit by insisting that Saddam Hussein was ready to negotiate a withdrawal. But indeed various offers—never taken up—were made.[83] And Arafat's claims to have worked before the invasion to arrange a settlement between Iraq and Kuwait, and afterwards (until the outbreak of war) to reach an Arab solution, as well as his claims that he had helped get hostages released,[84] were usually dismissed.

On the 1,000th day of the intifada, AIPAC launched an attack on the PLO. The *Near East Report* stated that the PLO, having said that it could only stand in the trench hostile to Zionism and its imperial allies, had placed itself squarely in the Iraqi camp; its ties were with neo-Nazis; its intifada was a jihad; it could not be a party to peace negotiations; it was attempting to impose a "reign of terror with measures more ruthless than the laws of the jungle, which characterize its ally Saddam Hussein."[85]

In noting and comparing international and American attitudes to the PLO and the Palestinian issue at this time, UN General Assembly Resolution 45168 of the 59th plenary meeting held on 6 December 1990 can be set alongside the *Near East Report* of 5 November 1990. In the UN Resolution, the General Assembly reiterated its previous positions. It criticised the "persistent policies and practices of Israel" and reaffirmed the need for a just and comprehensive settlement of the Arab/Israeli conflict, "the core of which is the question of Palestine." It repeated its call for an international conference based on Resolutions 242 and 338, with all parties to the conflict attending, including the PLO on an equal footing, plus the five permanent members of the Security Council; it called for Israel to withdraw from Palestinian territory and to dismantle the settlements.

Compare this with the *NER* article, "The End of Pan-Arabism." Here there is no criticism of Israel but rather an insistence on the isolation of the PLO: "The PLO has been the biggest loser in the current infighting. Arafat's embrace of Saddam Hussein has alienated his benefactors.... They have responded by cutting off funds for the PLO." Arafat's attempts to find a non-military solution to the Iraqi crisis were derided as "out-Saddaming Saddam" in "pitiful attempts to mediate a settlement." The PLO was presented as in no way representative of the Palestinians: "in the territories" Palestinians suffered, while the PLO leaders "live high on the hog in Tunis"—with a description of the PLO adviser who "peers disdainfully at a plate of grilled crevettes that don't meet his standards, and sends them back to the chef."

From the moment that Iraq invaded Kuwait, the PLO lost ground in American opinion. When war finally started, Israel was praised in the media (particularly the IVFR) while the Palestinians were constantly linked with their Iraqi "ally." Israel's behaviour in a war which she may have fomented and which helped her enormously was represented as exemplary. It was obvious that Israel benefited from the war; President Bush told the B'nai B'rith on 8 September 1992: "We stopped Saddam Hussein.... Israel, today, is safer: We didn't just talk about helping Israel, we did it."[86] And James Baker echoed the idea: "We have taken care of the greatest threat to Israel's security."[87] But Israel was commended for exposing her citizens to a first strike and refraining from response. Rep. Charles Schumer pressed for a UN resolution praising Israel, saying that "never before has a nation suffered a direct attack on its people and refrained from responding in the interests of world peace"; Israel constituted a "model of peaceful and faithful co-operation between nations." Rep. Charles Rangel insisted that "Israel has strengthened its moral position in the world order."[88] There was no mention of the reasons that might have prompted Israel's inactivity; she was presented as sacrificing herself for international peace (while at war). While numerous deaths were actually occurring, potential sufferings of Israelis were dramatically presented; the exposure of civilians to a gas attack was imagined in Biblical terms, while no mention was made of the fact that Palestinians had not been issued with gas masks.[89] The "courage and coolness" of Israeli citizens was praised and the continuing arrival of Soviet Jews was presented as an expression of commendable Zionist fervour.[90]

Meanwhile, the Palestinians were depicted as vindictive and ungrateful and Muslim, notwithstanding the fact that a large proportion of Palestinians are Christian: "Palestinians equipped with Israeli-supplied gas masks, were shouting 'Allah Akhbar'," and "Palestinians who prayed for a gas attack are now jubilant."[91] There was no mention of the rather natural fact that both Palestinians and Israelis cheered when shells hit the others' areas. Sen. Charles Grassley spoke of "Saddam and Arafat's [terrorism] campaign" and the *NER* insisted that the PLO was a terrorist organisation, emphasising its support for Iraq and its responsibility for intifada violence.[92]

What happened was a foregone conclusion: an upsurge in support for Israel and a dwindling of interest in the Palestinians among American Jews (and Americans generally). The *NER* of 20 May 1991 reported a poll taken by Americans Talk Issues, in which 55% of American respondents felt warmly towards Israel and only 8% towards the Palestinians. The *Jerusalem Post International* highlighted this by quoting a recent poll taken for the AJC's Institute on American Jewish-Israel relations by Steven Cohen (a "known dove," said *JPI*) and arguing that opinion had turned against the Palestinians.

Jewish attitudes in America have hardened considerably in the past two years. More American Jews now favor the expansion of settlements than do not; 83% believe that the PLO is "determined to destroy Israel" (as against 62% in 1989), and only 14% are concerned that continued rule of the administered territories is eroding the Jewish and humanitarian character of the State (as against 30% in 1988). All the findings clearly indicate that the Gulf War has made the community decidedly more hawkish on the Arab-Israeli conflict.[93]

The *Jerusalem Post International* was thus able to suggest that the American Jewish leaders whose positions had been more liberal had lost touch with the grass roots; it discredited the findings of other polls, and the acts of Jewish leaders. When it added that 71% of those polled said the U.S. should stop criticising Israel, it gave strength to the old argument that only those living in Israel could appreciate the dangers she was facing.

Thus the memory of the 1,000 days of intifada had been overlaid with new images; the sympathy for the Palestinians had been effaced by the Iraqi invasion and subsequent war. The intifada continued, as did the repression. The PLO had lost credit and funding. In the future lay the election of a new U.S. administration, President Bush having displeased the AIPAC by his initial refusal to grant loan guarantees to Israel unconditionally. Despite his September 1992 granting of $10 billion in loans guarantees without Israel having to stop settlement activity, his promise to urge other governments to put up another $10 billion, his promise that the usual $1.8 billion in military aid and $1.2 billion in civilian aid would continue and might even rise, his attempts to get Arab states to end their boycott of Israel, and his guarantee that Israel would remain militarily superior to the Arab states, Bush was depicted as pro-Arab, and 60% of Clinton's funding came from Jewish sources.[94] Maybe this was not only because of his stance on settlements but also because of his references to the "legitimate political rights of the Palestinian people" and the implementing of UN Resolutions 242 and 338. The *NER* issued a special supplement on the presidential primaries to show where Democratic candidates stood on Israel; (then) Governor Clinton adopted an extremely pro-Israel stance. He promised to provide $10 billion in unconditional loan guarantees, criticising the Bush administration's concern as to whether or not the settlements were legitimate or helpful. He declared that "Jerusalem is and should remain the capital of the State of Israel," "undivided." He opposed the idea of an international conference held under UN auspices. He thought Bush's criticism of Israel had set back the peace process[95] and that Bush had bullied Israel too long.[96] He was reported to be absolutely hostile to the creation of a Palestinian state.[97]

In the view of AIPAC president David Steiner, the Democrats were offering "the most pro-Israel platform in the Democratic Party's history."[98] The new Senate and House of Representatives were also heavily pro-Israel. So was President Clinton's Middle East team and his administration generally.[99]

And so, with little money, with the Arab world split, with the Soviet Union fallen, with the American Jewish community once again suspicious, with a strengthened Israeli lobby, and with an extremely pro-Israel U.S. administration in place, the PLO set out to negotiate peace with Israel.

NOTES

1. Brigadier Amnon Strashnov, quoted in *Jerusalem*, no. 67, December 1990, p. 14.
2. *Jerusalem*, no. 65, October 1990, pp. 31-34.
3. Lee O'Brien, American Jewish Organizations and Israel (Washington D.C.: Institute for Palestine Studies, 1986).
4. O'Brien, p.10, citing Melvin Urofsky.
5. I. Goldstein, *Transition Years: New York-Jerusalem 1960-1962* (Jerusalem: Rubin Mass, 1962), p. 173.
6. Goldstein, p. 118.
7. Goldstein, p. 196.
8. O'Brien, p. 11.
9. *Jerusalem Post International*, 7 March 1992. Fund-raising can produce large sums of money for Israel: *Jerusalem*, no. 57, February 1990, p. 22 reports that private American Jewish organisations donated over $3 billion per year. Deena Hurwitz, ed. *Walking the Red Line: Israelis in Search of Justice for Palestine* (New Society Publishers, 1992) describes how Israel gets $2-1/2 billion yearly in private American funds, $500 million from the sale of Israel Bonds and another $1 billion in private donations. O'Brien mentions various fund-raising bodies, pp. 107-146.
10. Rep. Mervyn Dymally in *The Link*, January/March 1992; Buchanan in *Al Fajr*, 31 August 1992.
11. O'Brien, p. 153.
12. *The Washington Report on Middle East Affairs*, November 1988.
13. O'Brien, p. 175.
14. Paul Findley, *Deliberate Deceptions: Facing the Facts About the US-Israeli Relationship* (New York: AMEU, 1993), reveals the type of methods used. Also an article by Paul A. Hopkins in *The Link*, January/March 1992 contains information and anecdotes.
15. O'Brien, p. 154.
16. O'Brien, p. 190, notes that from 1983-84, thirty-three pro-Israel PACs contributed about $3 million. *The Link* writes in its January/March 1992 issue that in the 1988 elections 78 pro-Israel PACs gave almost $6 million to 479 chosen candidates. The American Council for Judaism in its *Special Interest Report* for August

1988, vol. 19, no. 2, gives a list of 17 pro-Israel PACs contributing $1,442,069 to congressional campaigns by March 31 of that year.
   17. O'Brien, p.156, gives the story of Rudy Boschwitz, who sent out a fund-raising note with an endorsement from Sen. L. Weicker: "When it comes to raising money for political campaigns, every politician claims to be a friend of Israel."
   18. *Middle East International*, 9 July 1993; *Palestine*, no. 18, August 1993. An article in the *Jerusalem Post International*, 9 January 1993, had argued that the extent to which AIPAC provided the essential foundations for the U.S.-Israel relationship was not fully grasped by even Prime Minister Rabin.
   19. Mark Curtis, *The Ambiguities of Power: British Foreign Policy since 1945* (London: Zed Books, Ltd., 1995), p. 29.
   20. S.L. Spiegel, *The Other Arab-Israeli Conflict: Making America's Middle East Policy from Truman to Reagan* (Chicago: University of Chicago Press, 1985), p. 8.
   21. When it seemed that American Jews could not migrate to Israel as true Jews, fund-raising events were cancelled and criticism expressed. Where excuses had usually been made for Israel, "now nobody gives a damn about context," said A. Vorspan of the Union of American Hebrew Congregations. (*Jerusalem Post International*, December 3, 1988). Rabbi Alexander Schindler said: "The 'who-is-a-Jew' issue gave license for many to express their cumulative distress" (*Time*, April 3 1989).
   22. All taken from the American Council for Judaism's *Special Interest Report*, vol. 19, no. 2, August 1988.
   23. Taken from various American Jewish Committee reports, analyses and statements released during the period covered, also from the *Jerusalem Post*, 2 February 1988, and (then) AJC vice-president Ira Silverman in *Liberation*, 9 February 1989.
   24. Jerusalem *Post International*, 15 April 1989.
   25. *Jerusalem Post International*, 8 July 1989.
   26. D. Neff, "Eban Bashes the 'Friendly Columnists'," in *Middle East International*, 20 January 1989, p. 16.
   27. "Profile: Israel's dovish eagle," *The Observer*, 9 May 1993.
   28. Tom Segev, *The Seventh Million: The Israelis and the Holocaust* (New York: Hill and Wang, 1993), pp. 399-400.
   29. *Ibid.*, p. 400-401.
   30. Again, AJC literature for distribution during this period.
   31. G.E. Gruen and G. Wolf, "Continuing Turmoil in the West Bank and Gaza: Responses to the Current Crisis, Underlying Issues and Potential Solutions," AJC leaflet, April 1988, p. 7.
   32. *Jerusalem Post International*, 18 February 1989; *Time*, 3 April 1989 and 7 May 1990.
   33. "Summary of AJC Positions Relating to the Occupied Territories," 20 April 1988.
   34. AJC Statement on the Arab-Israel Peace Process, adopted by the National Executive Council, 1 November 1987.
   35. G.E. Gruen, "Rhetoric and Reality: Resolutions of the Palestine National Council," AJC leaflet, 18 November 1988.
   36. *Reuters Information Services Inc.*, 7 December 1988.
   37. American Council for Judaism's *Special Interest Report*, August 1988.
   38. "Jewish Spokesmen Divided on Arafat," *New York Times*, 8 December 1988.
   39. *Jerusalem News*, 30 October 1989.
   40. 87% in 1979, 77% in January 1989 (*Jerusalem Post International*, 18 February 1989).
   41. *American Arab Affairs*, Autumn 1989.

42. Israel-Diaspora Institute's October/November 1989 poll to which 780 out of over 1,310 American Jewish leaders replied (*International Herald Tribune*, 12 February 1990).
43. *Time*, 7 May 1990, p. 25.
44. *Jerusalem*, no. 57, February 1990, p. 23.
45. "Summary," AJC, 20 April 1988.
46. Gruen and Wolf, "Continuing Turmoil," 6 April 1988, pp. 9-10.
47. Gruen, "Rhetoric and Reality," 18 November 1988, p. 2.
48. *The Guardian*, 17 December 1988.
49. The 20% of 1979, or the 29% of the April 1988 *Los Angeles Times* poll.
50. *The Guardian*, 17 December 1988.
51. *Jerusalem Post International*, 15 April 1989.
52. *Al Fajr*, 8 June 1992.
53. *Jerusalem Post International*, 26 August 1989.
54. *International Herald Tribune*, 14 March 1990.
55. *Jerusalem*, no. 57, February 1990, p. 22.
56. *Time*, 7 May 1990, p. 26.
57. *Jerusalem Post International*, 22 April 1989.
58. *Jerusalem Post International*, 22 April 1989.
59. *Jerusalem*, no. 54, November 1989, p. 25.
60. *Jerusalem*, no. 54, November 1989, p. 26, quoting *Time*, 27 November.
61. All quotations from *Jerusalem Post International*, 21 July 1990.
62. *Jerusalem Post International*, 29 February 1992.
63. *Jerusalem Post International*, 9 July 1990.
64. *Jerusalem Post International*, 28 July 1990.
65. *Jerusalem Post International*, 9 July 1990.
66. *Jerusalem Post International*, 21 October 1991.
67. *Jerusalem Post International*, 26 May 1990.
68. *Jerusalem Post International*, 3 March 1990.
69. *Jerusalem*, no. 57, February 1990, p. 25.
70. Segev, p. 399.
71. *Newsweek*, 11 June 1990.
72. *Time*, 7 May 1990, p. 26. The *Jerusalem Post International*, 16 January 1993, quoted Barry Rubin as saying that Israel had pointed out the Iraqi "threat" to the U.S. and encouraged "U.S. fortitude" against Iraq. Zeev Eitan, of the Jaffee Center for Strategic Studies, believed that Iraq would always represent a threat to Israel (*Jerusalem Post International*, 23 January 1993).
73. J. Muravchik, "Patrick J. Buchanan and the Jews," in *Commentary*, vol. 91, 1, January 1991.
74. *Middle East International*, 31 August 1990, pp. 10, 11.
75. Rosenthal, "Won't Bush Level With The Troops" and Safire, "Assume the Iraqi Bomb Is Just Around the Corner," both in *International Herald Tribune*, 8 November 1990.
76. Neff, "Eban Bashes the 'Friendly Columnists'."
77. *Jerusalem*, no. 63, August 1990, pp. 4-5.
78. *L'autre journal*, January 1991.
79. Faisal Husseini and Jawid Al-Ghusain, in *Jerusalem*, no. 63, August 1990, p. 5.
80. *Jerusalem*, no. 63, August 1990, pp. 24-26.
81. *Jerusalem*, no. 66, November 1990, p. 5.
82. Paul Lalor, "The PLO's attitude to Saddam Hussein," in *Middle East International*, 31 August 1990, p. 30.
83. An Iraqi offer to withdraw in exchange for access to the Gulf and negotiations on the price of oil was presented to National Security Adviser Brent Scowcroft and National Security Council officials on 11 August; CIA chief Richard Helms

reported that "the U.S. government did not want to make a deal" (Alexander Cockburn, "The war goes on," *New Statesman and Society*, 5 April 1991, p. 15). The following week Iraq proposed a Mideast Peace Conference to settle all regional conflicts. On 3 January 1991 Iraq offered what the State Department called a "serious pre-negotiating offer" which "indicated the intention of Iraq to withdraw" (John Pilger, "Sins of Omission," *New Statesman and Society*, 8 February 1991, and "Liberal Triumphalism," *New Statesman and Society*, 15 March 1991). The refusal of negotiations was also described by Alexander Cockburn, "In for the Kill" (*New Statesman and Society*, 22 February 1991), John Gittings, "Saddam was Prepared to Agree Deal on Kuwait" (*Guardian*, 12 February 1991) and Martin Woollacott, "America's True Aim Laid Bare—To Remake Middle East" (*Guardian*, 16 February 1991).

84. Pierre Salinger, "Faltering Steps in the Sand," *Guardian*, 4 February 1991.
85. *Near East Report*, 8 October 1990.
86. *Le Monde*, 10 September 1992.
87. D. Neff, "The U.S., Iraq, Israel and Iran: Backdrop to War," in *Journal of Palestine Studies*, vol. xx, no. 4, Summer 1991. Neff describes Tarek Aziz's and Saddam Hussein's suspicions that Israel intended to attack Iraq's industrial and scientific sites, that Israel's supporters in Congress were constantly attacking Iraq, and that the U.S., Britain and Israel were plotting against her.
88. All quotations from the *Near East Report*, 25 February 1991.
89. *Jerusalem*, no. 65, October 1990, p. 22.
90. *Near East Report*, 28 January 1991.
91. *Near East Report*, 28 January 1991.
92. *Near East Report*, 25 February 1991, and 20 May 1991.
93. *Jerusalem Post International*, 21 October 1991.
94. *Middle East Labor Bulletin*, vol. 4, no. 2, Spring 1993, and *Middle East International*, 19 February 1993 on the media and financial support given to Clinton by Israel's supporters. Bush's remarks reported in *Al Fajr*, 20 April 1992.
95. *Near East Report*, 2 March 1992.
96. *Al Fajr*, 14 September 1992.
97. Michael Mandelbaum offered these views when he was addressing the Americans for Peace Now group during the New York Democrat Convention, *Jerusalem Post International*, 25 July 1992.
98. *Jerusalem Post International*, 25 July 1992.
99. *Middle East Labor Bulletin*, Spring 1993, especially pp. 23, 24, 25; *Middle East International*, 19 February 1993; *Jerusalem Post International*, 2 January 1993.

BIBLIOGRAPHY

PRIMARY SOURCES

GREAT BRITAIN:

Hansard
   vol. 248 (February 1931)
   vol. 326 (July 1937)
   vol. 347 (May 1939)
   vol. 424 (June 1946)
   vol. 426 (July 1946)
   vol. 460 (January 1949)

H.M. STATIONERY OFFICE:

League of Nations Mandate for Palestine, Cmd. 1785, 1922.
Report of the Commission on the Palestine Disturbances of August, 1929, Cmd. 3530, 1930.
Palestine Report on Immigration, Land Settlement and Development, by Sir John Hope-Simpson, Cmd. 3686, 1930.
Palestine Royal Commission, Cmd. 5479, 1937.
Palestine Statement of Policy, Secretary of State for the Colonies to Parliament, Cmd. 5513, 1937.
Palestine Statement of Policy, Secretary of State for the Colonies to Parliament, Cmd. 6019, 1939.
Report of the Anglo-American Committee of Enquiry, Cmd. 6808, 1946.
Anglo-American Agreement, Cmd. 7044 (July 1946-February 1947), containing extracts from the Herbert Morrison report of 1946, the constitutional proposals made by the Arab states 30 September 1946, and proposals by the British delegation to the Conference 7 February 1947).

HOUSE OF COMMONS:

Letter from Arthur J. Balfour to Lionel Walter Rothschild, 2 November 1917.

BOOKS:

Badeau, J.S. *The Middle East Remembered*. Washington: Middle East Institute, 1983.

Bell, G. *The Desert and the Sown*, 1907. Reprinted by Virago, 1985.

Bible, The Authorised King James Version.

BIBLIOGRAPHY 149

Church of Jesus Christ of the Latter Day Saints. *The Book of Mormon.* Deseret Enterprises, Ltd.

Cooke, A. "Harry S. Truman—A Study of a Failure," in *The Guardian*, 1 May 1948. Reprinted in *America Observed, From the 1940s to the 1980s.* New York: Alfred A. Knopf, 1989.

Glubb, Sir J. *The Changing Scenes of Life, Autobiography.* New York: Quartet Books, 1983.

Hodgkin, T. *Letters from Palestine, 1932-36.* Edited by E.C. Hodgkin. New York: Quartet Books, 1986.

Lawrence, T.E. Letters in R. Graves, *Lawrence and the Arabs.* Butler and Tanner Ltd., 1927.

Lloyd George, D. *War Memoirs*, vols. 1, 2. Odhams, 1933, 1938.

Stark, F. *East is West.* Century reprint 1986 of J. Murray, 1945.

SECONDARY SOURCES

BOOKS:

Allen, P.P. *Zionist Military Preparations for Statehood*, Ph.D. thesis for The American University, University Microfilm International, White Swan House, Godstone, 1975.

Banfield, E.C. and J.Q. Wilson. *City Politics.* New York: Vintage Books, 1966.

Black, E. *The Transfer Agreement.* Macmillan, 1984.

Blitzer, W. *Between Washington and Jerusalem: A Reporter's Notebook.* Oxford University Press, 1985.

Brown, G. *In My Way: The Political Memoirs of Lord George Brown.* Victor Gollancz Ltd., 1971.

Carmichael, J. *The Shaping of the Arabs.* George Allen and Unwin, 1969.

Chomsky, N. *The Fateful Triangle: The United States, Israel and the Palestinians.* London and Sydney: Pluto Press, 1983.

Cordesman, A.H. *The Arab-Israeli Military Balance and the Art of Operations*. University Press of America Inc., 1987.

Dallek, R. *Franklin D. Roosevelt and American Foreign Policy 1932-45*. New York: Oxford University Press, 1979.

Dimbleby, J. *The Palestinians*. Quartet Books Inc., 1980.

Encyclopaedia Judaica Year Book, 1986-7. Jerusalem: Keter Publishing House, Ltd., 1987.

Fromkin, D. *A Peace to End All Peace: Creating the Modern Middle East 1914-1922*. New York: Henry Holt and Co., 1989.

Giladi, G.N. *Discord in Zion*. London: Scorpion Publishing, 1990.

Glubb, Sir J. *Peace in the Holy Land—The Historical Analysis of the Palestine Problem*. Hodder and Stoughton, 1971.

Hallahmi, B. *The Israel Connection*. London: I.B. Tauris and Co. Ltd., 1988.

Halperin, S. *American Zionism: The Building of a Political Interest Group*, Ph.D. dissertation, Washington University, 1956.

_____. *The Political World of American Zionism*. Detroit: Wayne State University Press, 1961.

Hanauer, E.R. *An Analysis of Conflicting Jewish Positions Regarding the Nature and Political Role of American Jews with Particular Emphasis on Political Zionism*. Ph.D. thesis for the University of Idaho, University Microfilm International, White Swan House, Godstone, 1972.

Heller, Y. *LHI, Ideology and Politics 1940-1949*. Jerusalem: Keter Publishing House, Ltd., 1989.

Hourani, A. *The Emergence of the Modern Middle East*. Macmillan, 1981.

Hughes, B.B. *The Domestic Context of American Foreign Policy*. San Francisco: W.H. Freeman and Co., 1978.

Hurewitz, J.C. *The Middle East and North Africa in World Politics: A Democratic Record*, vol. 1. New Haven and London: Yale University Press.

Lerche, C.O. *Foreign Policy of the American People*, 3rd edition. Engleton Cliffs, New Jersey: Prentice-Hall, 1967.

Lilienthal, A. *The Zionist Connection*. New York: Dodd, Mead, 1978.

Louis, W.R. *Imperialism at Bay: The United States and the Decolonization of the British Empire 1941-1945*. New York: Oxford University Press, 1978.

———. *The British Empire in the Middle East 1945-1951*. Oxford: Clarendon Press, 1984.

Louis, W.R. and R.W. Stookey. *The End of the Palestine Mandate*. London: I.B. Tauris and Co. Ltd., 1986.

Marty, M.E. *Righteous Empire: The Protestant Experience in America*. New York: Dial Press, 1970.

———. *Pilgrims in Their Own Land*. Intercontinental Literacy, Arnold Heinemann, New Delhi, Agency of London, England, 1984.

McDowall, D. *Palestine and Israel*. London: I.B. Tauris and Co. Ltd., 1989.

Nederveen, J. *Israel's State Terrorism and Counterinsurgency in the Third World*. Near East Cultural and Educational Foundation with International Centre for Research and Public Policy, 1986.

Nevakivi, J. *Britain, France and the Arab Middle East 1914- 1920*. The Athlone Press, 1969.

Ovendale, R. *Britain, the United States and the End of the Palestine Mandate*. Royal Historical Society, Boydell Press, Woodbridge, Suffolk, 1989.

———. *The Origins of the Arab-Israeli Wars*. Longman, 1984.

Polenberg, R. *One Nation Divisible*. The Viking Press, 1980.

Polk, W.R. *The Arab World*. Harvard University Press, 1965; reprinted 1986.

Ray, J.L. *The Future of American-Israeli Relations*. The University Press of Kentucky, 1985.

Reich, B. *The United States and Israel*. New York: Praeger Specialist Studies, 1984.

Roberts, S.J. *Survival or Hegemony? Studies in International Affairs,* no. 20, John Hopkins University Press, Baltimore, Washington Centre of Foreign Policy Research School of Advanced Interest Studies, 1973.

Rubenberg, C.A. *Israel and the American National Interest.* University of Illinois Press, 1986.

Rubin, B. *The Great Powers in the Middle East 1941-1947 — The Road to the Cold War.* Frank Cass, 1980.

_____. *The Arab States and the Palestinian Conflict.* Syracuse University Press, 1981.

Rubin, J.A. *Partners in State-Building: American Jewry and Israel.* The Diplomatic Press Incorporated, 1967.

Safran, N. *Israel, the Embattled Ally.* Belknap/Harvard University Press, 1982.

Sanbar, E. *Palestine 1948: L'Expulsion, Institut des etudes palestiniennes.* Washington, D.C., 1984.

Sella, A. *Israel, the Peaceful Belligerent.* London, 1986.

Smith, P.A. *Palestine and the Palestinians 1876-1983.* London and Sydney: Croom Helm, 1984.

Spiegel, S.L. *The Other Arab-Israeli Conflict: Making America's Middle East Policy, from Truman to Reagan.* University of Chicago Press, 1985.

Stevens, R.P. *American Zionism and United States Foreign Policy 1942-1947.* New York: Pageant Press, 1962.

Stewart, D. *The Middle East: Temple of Janus.* Hamish Hamilton, 1972.

Stivens, W. *America's Confrontation with Revolutionary Change in the Middle East, 1948-1983.* New York: St. Martin's Press, 1986.

Touval, S. *The Peace Brokers: Mediators in the Arab-Israeli Conflict, 1948-1979.* Princeton University Press, 1982.

Urofsky, M.I. *American Zionism from Herzl to the Holocaust.* Garden City, New York: Anchor Press/Doubleday, 1975.

Wilson, E.M. *Decision on Palestine: How the United States Came to Recognise Israel.* Hoover Institution Press, Stanford University, 1979.

Wilson, Sir J.H. *The Chariot of Israel: Britain, America and the State of Israel.* George Weidenfeld & Nicholson Ltd., and Michael Joseph Ltd., London, 1981.

Wyman, D.S. *Abandonment of the Jews.* New York: Pantheon Books, 1985.

United Nations Publications:
The Right of Return of the Palestinian People, 1978.
The Right of Self-Determination of the Palestinian People, 1979.
Acquisition of Land in Palestine, 1980.
The United Nations and the Question of Palestine, 1985.

ARTICLES:

Baumel, T. Extract from 1981 thesis, *Jerusalem Post International*, 4 November 1989.

Forbes, J. "Racism: A Review," *Explorations in Ethnic Studies*, January 1982.

The Link, vol. 16, 4 November 1983: Various articles on fundamentalism.

Neff, D. "Palestine, Truman and America's Strategic Balance," *American-Arab Affairs*, no. 25, summer 1988.

Parker, T. "America Foreign Policy. 1945-1976," *Facts on File*, Inc., New York, 1980.

Pipes, D. "Israel, America and Arab Delusions," *Commentary*, vol. 91, 3, March 1991, published by the American Jewish Committee.

Rockaway, R.A. "Scoundrel Time," *Jerusalem Post International*, 5 May 1990.